TIMELINE

TIMELINE

T. M. Shine

A month in the life of a guy who refuses to have
money taken out of his paycheck for United Way; a
guy who always eats lunch alone; a guy so fascinated
with time that he documents the way he spends it—
every day, every hour, every minute, every second

Andrews McMeel
Publishing

Kansas City

For my people

01 02 03 04 05 RDH 10 9 8 7 6 5 4 3 2 1

Library of Congress Cataloging-in-Publication Data
Shine, T. M.
Timeline : a month in the life of a guy who won't have money
taken out of his paycheck for United Way, a guy who always
eats lunch alone, a guy so fascinated with time that he documents the way he spends it—every day, every hour, every
minute, every second / T.M. Shine.
    p. cm.
ISBN 0-7407-1417-1 (pbk.)
    1. American wit and humor. I. Title.

PN6162 .S4979 2001
818'.607—dc21   00-061786

Book design by Holly Camerlinck

Acknowledgments

A special thank you to Michael Farver and City Link for allowing me a weekly forum. Much appreciation to Patty Rice, Emilio Perez, Jennifer Fox, Ernie Pheirim, Skot Olsen, Michael Koretzky, and Sal Galan. Much sympathy to Johnny "99" Hughes, Dave Warm, and Danny Shine for being bottomless pits of material. And thanks always to Chris, Robin Doussard, Marjorie Shine, Mark Gauert, Stu Purdy, Dave Barry, Greg "The Don" Carannante, Tom Shroder, Al Hart, Pete Shine, and Mike Bartolillo.

Introduction

I think it was the great Billy Joel who sang, "These are not the best of times, but they're the only times I've ever known."

And I think it was my cousin Jimmy who, on a Tuesday at 4:14 P.M., said, "Turn that crap off. I hate Billy Joel."

But anyway, time has always been one of my favorite subjects. I love the way we document it the second we enter this world. Length: 21 inches. Weight: 7 pounds, 9 ounces. Time of birth: 3:20 A.M.

Could there be any more useless information than the time you were born?

Well, that's how this began. I decided I would start documenting all the useless information instead of the important stuff. All that daily debris that we often allow to just whip by us without a second thought, I would get out a pen and make note of it.

When I first started doing this on yellow legal pads people would look over my shoulder, see all the dots and numbers, and say things like, "Are those psalms?"

I'm not very sociable, so I would say things such as "Go away." But, in an odd way, some of the moments that I log could certainly have the same impact as psalms. There are nuggets of enlightenment that expose themselves, like the fact that ordering a dozen doughnuts is a metaphor for life. And occasionally something very disturbing is discovered, like when the subject of a certain doctor's all-night liposuction practices came up and a guy who rarely talks to me said at exactly 10:41 A.M.: "Where does all the fat go?

"They're doing so many operations you know the doctors aren't paying a biohazard company to haul off that kind of quantity of fat," he continued. "No, he's putting it in the trunk of his car and dumping half of it himself. Hefty bags of fat. Sooner or later it's going to end up in the water system. One glass of water will be equal to eating two Big Macs. Eventually there'll be some big *60 Minutes* exposé like with Love Canal . . . only it'll be Fat Canal. Yeah, babies being born weighing forty pounds and . . ."

And you get the idea. There is a lot of stuff that is worth documenting for no reason at all and that's what I've decided to put all my efforts into.

In the course of this endeavor I have found that everything in every day is different, except for two things.

1. I always end up eating lunch alone.
2. And every time the boss asks me if I want to have money taken directly out of my paycheck for United Way my answer is always: "No F---ing way."

What we have in this book is a month of my life and a little bit of yours, I suspect. Although I did have a woman tell me recently that my biggest misconception was thinking that other people would identify with my life. "You know, not everybody has an ex-con move into their house," she said.

"Go away," I said. And she did, so I don't have to worry about that anymore.

Just two more things because I wanted to end this exactly at 1:14.

1. As I have learned—and you will see—it is a mistake to document one's life so closely. I do not recommend it.
2. Please don't confuse this with a diary. It is so much less. It is fleeting thoughts squished together and jammed into a freezer bag like chopped leftovers. It is the bottom of your shoe and everything that has stuck to it all day. It is . . .

1:14 A.M.

T. M. S.
Thursday, 1:14 A.M.

A Monday

*"Up and away, got a big day, gotta run, run,
yeah, yeah . . ."*

—HARRY NILSSON

7:33 A.M.: Read horoscope. It says, "All your favorite relatives are coming to visit." Who the hell has favorite relatives?

8:25 A.M.: "Got a big day ahead of you?" neighbor asks as I'm rushing to the car. Actually, I say, I'm hoping for a small day.

9:40 A.M.: An attractive woman from the neck up smiles and waves to me as I pull into the parking garage at work. I don't know who she is but appreciate the gesture.

9:55 A.M.: People in office are already talking about lunch. Someone I consider a lunch expert once told me that if you don't want your bosses to know that you're taking an extra-long lunch you should leave around 11:00. "No one ever notices if you're early going to lunch, only if you're late coming back," he said.

10:10 A.M.: A close friend calls to ask me if I will help her steal her anorexic roommate's Stairmaster after work. "It's bad enough that she's a vegetarian that doesn't eat vegetables," she says. "If she doesn't stay off that Stairmaster she's going to either die or disappear." No can do, I say.

10:25 A.M.: I'm at my desk, making up odometer readings for my expense report (using a lot of 8s this week), when a woman I don't immediately recognize strides up. "Oh, there you are," she says. I nod in agreement.

10:27 A.M.: "I just wanted to let you know I didn't mean to wave to you this morning. You have the same car as a friend of mine. It was a mistake," she says, huffing and puffing like she's been on an exhaustive search through the building. "You tracked me down to take back a wave? Is that what it's come to in our society?" I ask. "Yes," she says.

10:28 A.M.: Take it, I say.

11:00 A.M.: Go to lunch and eat alone.

12:44 P.M.: Get back from lunch.

12:45 P.M.: "Aren't you going to take a lunch today?" the boss says, stopping by my desk. Maybe later if I can get caught up here, I say.

1:10 P.M.: Phone rings. "If we can just get the Stairmaster out of there it would buy her some time," the voice says. "Please help me. Think of it like taking a gun away from a child. You should have seen her all dressed up this morning and heading to work like nothing's wrong. She looked like Buddy Ebsen in a Jacqueline Smith pantsuit. Please!" No can do, I say.

1:11 P.M.: "Why?" she demands. What do you want me to do, I say, spell out for you—minute by minute—how much goes on in my own life each day? I haven't got the time for that. Good-bye.

1:16 P.M.: Boss stops by desk, looks at the legal pad on my desk, and says, "What's with all the numbers and dots?" Those are times, I say. "What's with all the times?" he says. I'm spelling out—minute by minute—what goes on in my own life each day. "Oh," he says.

2:10 P.M.: Seriously think about taking that second lunch.

2:30 P.M.: I just read an article about a guy who is illiterate so that when he writes his name he doesn't write it. He draws it. I start practicing drawing my name instead of writing it and before I know it it's time to go home.

5:32 P.M.: Two maintenance workers are in the elevator. "You would think that if you were a postal worker you wouldn't go nuts on principle. You know, just so you wouldn't become a cliché," one says to the other. "When you're that upset," the other says, "you don't even care about clichés."

5:34 P.M.: As I'm pulling out of the parking garage I pass you-know-who and give her a big wave. She gives me the finger.

5:50 P.M.: Hear news flash on the radio about Puff Daddy getting caught having sex on the beach but Puffy's publicist is denying it. "I know for a fact," she says, "that Puffy hates sand."

6:28 P.M.: When I get home a neighbor greets me in my own driveway. "What's new?" she says. Puffy hates sand, I say.

6:50 P.M.: We decide to go out to dinner. We're at the restaurant and the wife orders a hot roast beef sandwich. The waitress says, "You're going to have to sign for it." Huh? "If you want meat you have to sign for it."

6:53 P.M.: After a three-minute silence I ask why, but the waitress says it's too complicated. (I find out later it had something to do with a certain transport company they use violating state policies.) I don't want anyone in our family eating meat we have to sign for, I tell my wife. But she insists. "I'll get the paperwork," the waitress says.

7:01 P.M.: "Don't get so upset. We haven't been out for a while, maybe you have to sign for meat everywhere now," my wife says, trying to calm me down. I'm not that upset, I say. I still care about becoming a cliché.

7:03 P.M.: I tell her to draw her name on the meat contract instead of write it so at least if anything happens maybe the signature won't hold up in court and we can still get a small settlement for her funeral expenses or whatever.

8:15 P.M.: Rented *Things to Do in Denver When You're Dead* video on the way home. Chris Walken is a quadriplegic mob leader and I can't get over the part where he commands his henchmen to cross his legs for him. That's so cool. I keep playing that part over and over while my wife is in the bathroom.

9:55 P.M.: Call my father, who eats out all the time. "No, son, we've never had to sign for meat."

10:42 P.M.: Ask wife to cross my legs for me. Please, it's been a long day. *Please.*

11:06 P.M.: Watch TV until I wake up to go to bed.

11:18 P.M.: As I'm climbing into bed my wife says, "Your Uncle John called while you were asleep watching TV. Said he might be coming down." Oh, great. He's my favorite relative.

DAY 2

Intermittent Thoughts

*"I'm living in a time of inconvenience at
an inconvenient time."*

—NANCI GRIFFITH

8:10 A.M.: "Don't forget to get those papers notarized today," my wife says. Don't we have a friend who's a notary like everybody else does? I ask. "We don't have any friends," she says.

8:12 A.M.: "Hey, did you see Garth Brooks on cable over the weekend?" a neighbor yells over. "It was unscrambled for everybody!" I prefer my Garth Brooks scrambled, I say.

8:33 A.M.: On the interstate on way to work. A few months ago, I was very proud when I found a car at the right price with absolutely no options but now it's raining lightly and I just realized I have no intermittent wipers.

8:34 A.M.: Turn on wipers.

8:34:07 A.M.: Turn off wipers.

8:34:22 A.M.: Turn on wipers.

8:34:44 A.M.: I can't live like this.

9:50 A.M.: Enter a discussion in lobby about how many miracles you would need on an application for sainthood. "It's going to have to be an awful lot to rule out all the chiropractors," the guy who thinks he's Jay Leno says.

10:04 A.M.: Sitting on everyone's desks at work is a new black bag with the company logo on it. Every year we get something. Last year it was spatulas. Anyway, it's an odd size—too small for travel, too big for a personal bag. It says "duffel" on the tag but I always thought a duffel bag was something you could throw all your crap in and head home on leave with. This bag just doesn't seem Greyhound-worthy.

10:23 A.M.: Look up *duffel* in the dictionary.

10:41 A.M.: Cousin calls to tell me he just went to the doctor to get a referral to see a therapist. "I waited for thirty minutes and then he sees me for one minute and starts writing a prescription for Prozac. Says it'll save me time. But I told him I don't want to be medicated. I don't want to be somebody that's on something. I just need someone to talk to. Is that too much to ask?" I gotta go, I say.

11:18 A.M.: Wife calls to tell me that when I brought stuff in from Costco, the warehouse club, over the weekend, I accidentally put the three-pack of toothpaste in the freezer with the 210-pack of breakfast sausages. "Because of you," she says, "our toothpaste is frozen."

11:50 A.M.: Tell supervisor that I may be a little late coming back from lunch. I have to get something notarized. "You really don't have any friends, do you?" he says.

12:10 P.M.: Pass huddle of eight people smoking in front of the building. They're giggling, engaged in passionate conversation and patting each other on the back. I bet I'd have friends if I smoked.

12:15 P.M.: Eat lunch alone.

12:52 P.M.: Go to credit union to get money. The gentleman in front of me looks up awkwardly and says, "I went to this Italian theme party over the weekend and brought sangria. Everybody laughed at me. I didn't know it was from Spain. Big deal, anyway."

12:53 P.M.: Ahh . . . (I assume the man is in pain, possibly suffering from pennant fever, and I want to say something but I'm not really good at non sequiturs.) Ahh . . . Because of me . . . our toothpaste is frozen."

12:53:02 P.M.: "Next."

1:15 P.M.: On the way to the notary's office I see what must be a Haitian woman coming across the parking lot at Sears with a boxed twenty-seven-inch color TV on her head. She's making good time and reaching into her purse for her car keys like it's nothing.

1:30 P.M.: "Do you mind if I go first?" says a woman rushing into the notary's office. "I'm not in a big hurry but I've got a friend in the car and she'll go nuts if I leave her out there too long." Is she on something? I inquire. "Worse," she says. "She's off something."

1:33 P.M.: "Do you know how much it costs to have something notarized?" the woman asks me. I'm not sure but I think it's kind of like when you get a flat tire fixed, I say. Sometimes the guy just wants like four dollars to stuff in his pocket to buy lunch at Arby's and other times they make you go into the office and sign papers, get a two-page receipt, and pay $13.76.

1:35 P.M.: Woman goes into notary's cubicle and quickly comes out. "Arby's money," she says, whisking past me.

1:36 P.M.: Notary has a *Fargo* snow globe on her desk. There's an overturned car in there and a body. Very bloody. I shake it and in the time it takes two flakes to settle on Marge's expectant tummy I'm notarized and on my way.

2:40 P.M.: Cousin calls to vent that it's uncaring people like me who make other people need medication. He's blabbering. "I don't know how your conscience lives with you," he says. Where's it gonna go, I say.

3:40 P.M.: Wife calls to tell me she's going to get home early and make baked ziti. Great, I say, I love Italian. I'll bring the sangria.

4:10 P.M.: Boss stops by my desk. "With all those times and stuff you keep writing down, what do you do, just keep track of the important stuff?" he asks. No, no, don't worry, I say. This is strictly for the unimportant stuff. "Okay, I just wanted to make sure," he says.

5:01 P.M.: People in office are trying to see if they can fit anything in those bags before taking them home. Some are trying to use it to smuggle out last year's spatulas but the handles that say "Read Us With Breakfast" keep sticking out.

5:15 P.M.: I crumple up some paper and pack the duffel like a new purse so it has some shape to it, then move out. Heading home on leave, I nod to passersby in the hallways.

6:20 P.M.: On interstate. There was a time, not that long ago, that I would use this commute to relax, sit back, and think about things like how we should accept new cultures to our shores (especially if they can teach us how to avoid the package pickup guys at Sears); how we are so cynical that as long as we are the audience there can be no more miracles; how my tooth-paste is currently thawing on the windowsill. But now . . .

6:20:08 P.M.: Drop . . . drop . . .

6:20:08 P.M.: I no longer have the time.

DAY 3

Talkin' 'bout an Evolution

"Do you really not understand it's a brand new world?"

—ANDY STEIN

7:25 A.M.: All my teeth wake up estranged from each other. Something is out of whack. It used to be that when I bit down everybody was shaking hands. Now, strangers on a bus.

8:55 A.M.: By coincidence I have a teeth cleaning scheduled for this morning. All these years, Natalie, the hygienist, has been asking me, "Anything bothering you?" and I always say, No.

9:02 A.M.: Yes.

9:03 A.M.: Like most hygienists, Natalie likes to play dentist. She circles. "Could be TMJ. Have you been grinding your teeth in your sleep?" she asks. I don't know, how would I know, I must do a lot of things in my sleep. I always wake up tired. Is that what this is, TMJ? "I don't know," she says. "I'm not a dentist."

9:04 A.M.: Hands me pamphlet on TMJ, which is mostly about the shifting of one's jaw.

9:06 A.M.: She flips down her plastic face shield and moves in close for the cleaning. Ordinarily at this time, I would gaze in at her dark red lipstick and the tiny mole on her left cheek and fantasize that she's a Russian cosmonaut trying to climb into my pod on the last night of a six-month stint at the space station. But not today.

9:15 A.M.: I can't stop thinking that this is a positive thing. On the Discovery Channel they're always showing how man's jaw evolved over the different prehistoric eras. Maybe this is just an evolution of sorts. Perhaps they're just shifting on their way to becoming superior teeth. Maybe a year from now I'll be mincing dry sirloin in half the time and eliminating flossing all together. I'll have self-cleaning teeth.

9:27 A.M.: "Rinse," Natalie says.

9:28 A.M.: Natalie, this could just be a sign that my whole being is evolving, I say. Here's a free toothbrush, she says.

9:29 A.M.: Receptionist tells me the dentist has an opening Thursday so I can get my jaw X-rayed. That won't be necessary, I say.

9:30 A.M.: On the way out I feel a bit superior as I pass others in the waiting room.

9:31 A.M.: In the car I realize I have felt smarter lately, I've just been ignoring it because I don't know what to do with it.

10:02 A.M.: Woman on the radio is saying that some baseball star who just arrived from Cuba shouldn't have to have a translator in the locker room since sportscasters always ask the same questions and players always give the same answers. "All he needs is a few phrases like 'It was a team effort,' and he's covered," she says. Makes sense.

10:20 A.M.: There's a clown in the lobby at work. He's right in front of the elevators. Go back to sit in my car for an hour.

10:35 A.M.: Wait a second. The old me would wait out a clown. The new, evolving me would figure something out.

10:55 A.M.: Twelve flights. That's a lot of stairs.

11:02 A.M.: "Did you know John Denver was a sniper in the Vietnam war?" a coworker says. "You never really know someone until they're dead."

11:15 A.M.: An old classmate calls to tell me he wants Fridays to mean something again. "I miss that feeling of cashing my paycheck and picking up a six-pack. Now I drink every night and I've got direct deposit, but that's all going to change. I canceled my direct deposit and I'm staying dry until Friday. You with me on this one?" Oh, on any other day I'd be with you, my brother, but you just happen to have caught me in the middle of an evolution of sorts and I can't go backward, not even for a six-pack.

11:20 A.M.: Mention to coworker that I'm in the process of moving up the evolutionary chain. "Well, let me know when you catch up to me," he says.

12:15 P.M.: Go to lunch and eat alone. Notice that I now have much less trouble putting my tuna kit together.

1:05 P.M.: On the way back to the office I run into a reporter from the daily newspaper that operates out of our basement. What are you workin' on? I ask. "Oh," she says excitedly, "I'm doing a story on Awareness Month." Awareness of what? "Ahh . . ."

1:06 P.M.: This could get to be a drag—always being smarter than everyone else, putting people on the spot, mocking my inferiors. I can only assume that I will reach a point of such superiority that I will become humble. At this rate I could end up a Buddhist. Today could be my seven years in Tibet.

1:08 P.M.: Maybe I would go back for a twelve-pack.

1:10 P.M.: We get a report that management is going to be washing employees' cars next week. "Last week they had them serving us lunch," a coworker says. "They keep calling it employee appreciation, but I think they're just looking for things for them to do." Being humble, I try not to laugh.

2:10 P.M.: Old classmate calls again. "Forget it. I can't wait until Friday. I'm going to drink tonight," he says.

2:51 P.M.: Wife calls to tell me the good news is my Uncle John decided not to come. The bad news is our niece in rural Port St. Lucie wants to know if her twenty-two-year-old boyfriend can stay with us. "She said it would just be for a couple of weeks so he can get a job. All they have up there is McDonald's," my wife says. So what's wrong with McDonald's? I ask. "They fired him." Ahh, I'd love to help, but fast food is usually the last stop, isn't it? I don't think there's anywhere to go once you've been fired from McDonald's.

2:52 P.M.: "Oh, and I guess he's had some trouble with the law," she says. He's not an ex-con, is he? I ask. "I think that's what they call it."

3:12 P.M.: Find out that was the United Way clown in the lobby. I know it won't be long before someone will be coming around to say, "Are you going to donate this year? You can have it taken right out of your check so you won't even miss it."

Oh, I'll miss it.

3:13 P.M.: This United Way thing is really a dilemma. In the past I have taken the attitude that it's a joke that the company tries to make you feel bad about not having money taken out of your check when they haven't put anything in your check in the past five years. But now that I'm on a higher plane that seems petty. I should give.

3:16 P.M.: Nah.

3:40 P.M.: Everyone in the office is watching the new Game Show Network. Rerun of 1970s *Newlywed Game* is on. Those hairdos. As a species we really have evolved over the past couple of decades.

5:10 P.M.: Somebody has a copy of the original *South Park Xmas* short that only circulated on the Internet years ago. "Come see," they say. At this stage of my evolution I don't think it would be prudent to . . . "Come on, Jesus wrestles Santa Claus." Well, maybe just a peek.

6:12 P.M.: When I get home I notify my wife of my unbelievable growth both physically and mentally. "You laugh," I say. "But it's just a matter of time before the rest of me catches up to my teeth."

6:32 P.M.: It's spreading. I suddenly feel like finishing that book on quasi-economics that my brother-in-law gave me. Can't remember where I left off. "You read the title," my wife says.

6:33 P.M.: Make an entry in my diary: Everything in my life is about to change, except I'm still not going to give to United Way.

6:37 P.M.: Did I mention that I think I'm a Buddhist now? I shout to my wife.

7:20 P.M.: Old classmate calls again. Sounds drunk. "Can't believe I'm gonna have to go to the f---ing bank on Friday!"

9:15 P.M.: TV no longer interests me but I can't think of anything else to do.

10:40 P.M.: Take out my new toothbrush and try it out. It's a very sophisticated Oral B, but when I finish brushing it won't fit in the holder. What kind of half-assed advancement is this?

10:42 P.M.: I cram it but the end is too broad. It won't stand up. I lay it down next to the other brushes. It looks pitiful but I know how it feels to be the best, brightest, and most sophisticated thing around in a world that can't keep up with you.

10:43 P.M.: I go lie down.

DAY 4

Full Mental Jacket

"I'm coming, Elizabeth, I'm coming!"

—FRED SANFORD

10:11 A.M.: Big Boss (BB) comes in and directs everyone to the center ring—where he is standing—to tell us he wants to have one-on-one lunches with everyone. He doesn't want to just be this guy in a suit who stops in once in a while.

10:12 A.M.: "We never see the whole suit," someone pipes up. "Well, I leave the jacket on my chair upstairs," BB says.

10:12:06 A.M.: "Can we see it?" someone asks. "See," BB says, "this is what I'm talking about. I want to get to know you and I want you to know everything about me. I want you to know how I feel about the future of this company, about the revenues we need to generate, our place in the community, the big picture . . ."

10:13 A.M.: "I think he's talking about the Kwan, like in *Jerry Mcguire*," someone mumbles. "The Korporate Kwan."

10:13:12 A.M.: I may be a little paranoid but I immediately think this whole thing is just camouflage to hide the fact that I'm the only one he wants to have lunch with so he can get me to confess to something I've only thought about doing.

10:13:44 A.M.: "And I want to know about each of you," BB keeps rolling. "I mean, I don't even know where everybody's from. You could have been raised on the Mississippi Delta for all I know," he says, pointing at one employee.

10:14 A.M.: "I wasn't," she says.

10:14:13 AM.: "I was," says our resident yes-man, who everyone knows was raised in Orlando.

10:14:44 A.M.: "And I want you to know all those little things about me," BB says. "I want us to get under each other's skin. I want to get up close and personal. I want you to smell me."

10:15 A.M.: Okay, everybody nods.

10:17 A.M.: BB tells us his assistant will call each of us individually to schedule our lunches. "Do we have to wait until our lunch to see the jacket?" someone asks. "We'll see if we can work something out," he says.

10:20 A.M.: As BB walks out, new guy is just coming in late and is wearing what look like golf shoes. "Soft cleats," he says, digging into the carpet and doing a 360. "I don't even golf," he says. "But they make me feel wily."

11:02 A.M.: Get a solicitation in the mail to buy four uncut versions of *Sanford and Son*. It must have just reached sitcom classic status after all these years. "Build your own private library of the funniest man in junk," it says. I can picture ol' Fred clutching his chest and the tidbits in the ad are titillating ("remember him telling his son Lamont the woman he wants to marry is a 'King Kong in bloomers'"), but I keep hesitating every time my hand goes to check the box next to: "YES—I want to salvage big laughs with *Sanford and Son*."

11:18 A.M.: Workers are discussing how they're going to order big expensive meals with BB. Talk of lobster and filet mignon is in the air. "You know, I've only eaten fake crabmeat," one coworker says.

11:32 A.M.: Cousin calls to tell me the woman he double-cheesed is breaking up with him. This was the woman who was so special two weeks ago that when he was making her a Kraft Macaroni & Cheese dinner he ripped open a second box and used an extra pouch of cheese in one batch. "It was so cheesy. She loved it. How could she leave me after I did something that special?" he groans. Forget her, I say. She's a King Kong in bloomers.

11:41 A.M.: BB's assistant calls down to notify employees that they can start going up in groups of three to see the suit jacket.

11:45 A.M.: "Fred Sanford establishes new comedy records for faked heart attacks, sudden illnesses, and instant brushes with death. And he's hilarious every time," the brochure says. Can't argue with that.

11:55 A.M.: First group comes back from jacket field trip. "We just missed it," they say.

12:02 P.M.: Marketing guys stop in front of workstation. "I can only talk about this in the abstract," the first guy says. Nearby coworker and I are all ears. We've never actually heard anyone talk in the abstract before.

12:02:15 P.M.: "So this is it in a nutshell . . ." the guy begins. So much for the abstract, we say, going back to work.

12:18 P.M.: Second jacket troop comes back. "His assistant said it was just there a second ago but he must have grabbed it for an important meeting or something," they say. Some employees are starting to think the jacket doesn't exist. "I don't want to eat with someone who lies about something like that, not even for real crabmeat."

12:28 P.M.: The scent of surf and turf is still in the air when regular boss announces that the bad news is that BB's assistant just called and it seems that ten minutes after BB left us he became so overwhelmed by the thought of having exhaustingly time-consuming lunches with everyone that it's been changed to just "Snack Time with the Big Boss." The good news is: The jacket is back if anyone wants to shoot up there.

12:31 P.M.: Guy who already has his lunch with the boss scheduled for today wants to know if his lunch is canceled or if he'll be grandfathered in.

12:40 P.M.: Last crew that went to see the jacket never came back, and regular boss is getting uneasy. Sends rescue party to go up and find them. "Be careful," he says. "The air is thin up there."

12:45 P.M.: Guy who was grandfathered in heads out to meet BB for lunch. On his way out he looks down at a small group of people trying to think of what the most expensive snack they could have with the boss would be. "I've got one," someone says. "After Eight Mints. They're imported."

12:47 P.M.: There's been so much talk about lunch I decide to skip lunch. I'm full.

1:41 P.M.: Grandfathered-in returns from having lunch with BB and everyone bombards him with questions:
"What did he smell like?"
"Ball bearings."
"Where did you tell him you were born and raised?"
"The Deep South."
"Did you have real crabmeat?"
"The waitress said there's no such thing as real crabmeat."

2:01 P.M.: After commotion I try to get some telling details. Did you confess to anything you've only thought about doing? I ask. "I'm not sure," he says. "He was talking in the abstract."

2:27 P.M.: Some may never be found, but about eleven people come back from seeing the jacket.
"What did it smell like?"
"Armor-All."

3:15 P.M.: Assistant calls asking who wants to volunteer for today's snack time at 3:30.

3:33 P.M.: The first snacker is back. After Eight Mints? "Pringles," she says. What did he smell like? "Pringles."

3:59 P.M.: BB has had a change of heart about the snack thing. Some employees filed a complaint that it's unfair that one person got lunch and twenty-two others just get a snack. He doesn't want to have more lunches because it is really hard to get to know people while they're eating anyway, but his assistant is faxing a list titled "Activity Time with the Boss" that should take between twenty and twenty-five minutes each.

4:02 P.M.: I'm just not sure I can take Aunt Esther. She was so meddlesome.

4:04 P.M.: Two-page list arrives. Includes stuff like fourteen-mile Water Taxi Ride, Fully Clothed Massages, Bocce Ball, Reading Inscriptions on Donated Bricks on Riverwalk, etc.

4:06 P.M.: "All right! Sand art," someone shouts.

4:10 P.M.: So many choices. I check "YES—I want to salvage big laughs with *Sanford and Son.*"

4:13 P.M.: Double-cheese calls me. "I'm boiling up the macaroni," he says. "I'm going to just eat them cheeseless to remind myself that people in this world are completely unappreciative." Come on, you gotta put something on them. "No, I don't want this meal to go down easy. This is just to teach myself a lesson." Come on, a little butter, something. "Nope, I'm just eatin' 'em wet."

4:16 P.M.: Uh-oh. Activities have been retracted. Some kind of insurance problem. BB does not want to drag this on and distract us from our work, so he wants to go back to the one-on-one lunch plan. Only he wants to lunch with everyone on the same day. Starting tomorrow.

4:17 P.M.: First lunch will be at 9:15, then 10:23, 11:04, and so on, his assistant notifies us.

4:18 P.M.: "Nine-fifteen!" someone yells. "Even over-crowded schools don't start lunches until ten."

4:18:07 P.M.: There are a million questions as everyone starts hustling toward the door. Is he actually going to eat lunch ten times in one day?

4:19 P.M.: "Hey, where's everybody going?" our regular boss says. "We've got a monster workload this week. I need people to stay late."

4:19:05 P.M.: "Are you kidding?" the wily guy in golf shoes says. "We have to get up early for lunch."

DAY 5

All for One, One for All

"Two can be as bad as one."

—HARRY NILSSON

6:12 A.M.: "Maybe you should get up and see what that noise is?" my wife says. What for? I say. I know it's a criminal. We invited him to live here.

6:15 A.M.: We're only into Day 2 of having my Port St. Lucie niece's twenty-two-year-old ex-con boyfriend stay with us and already I'm having second and third thoughts. "Just go check," my wife says. "Maybe it's a criminal we don't know." If it is, should I invite him to stay?

6:22 A.M.: He's working out. On my living room furniture. Everything is rearranged. Tables are pushed back. Chairs are in the center of the room with backs facing each other so he can do some kind of pull-ups. One end of the couch is propped up with books and he's lying on it (shirtless as always) doing sit-ups. He's turned a butter-leather couch into an inclined bench. And he's so upset that I caught him doing this that he rises up, looks me in the eye, and says, "Eleven . . . twelve."

6:22:01 A.M.: No! No! I say. You're not turning my living room into a makeshift prison yard . . . workout . . . center . . . type . . . place. Ahhh! This is not your day in the yard. Go to your room.

6:23 A.M.: Go back to bed. Realize I don't even know his last name. What if he robs us and police come and we can't even give them the name of the person who's been living with us for several days. How stupid are we going to look then? I ask myself.

6:23:01 A.M.: No response.

6:35 A.M.: I can't sleep without knowing the last name of the criminal working out in my living room.

6:36 A.M.: Get up. Hey, I say, what's your last name?

6:37 A.M.: Go back to bed.

7:22 A.M.: Sleep soundly for forty-five minutes. That's the kind of peace you're afforded when you know the last name of the criminal working out in your living room.

8:15 A.M.: Get up to take shower.

8:17 A.M.: There's too many bottles in here, I shout from the shower. Why can't I have my shampoo and conditioner in one? People do that.

8:18 A.M.: "What happened? You mistake the conditioner for the shampoo again?" my wife assumes.

8:18:12 A.M.: Yes.

8:19 A.M.: I hate when this happens. It's like when you go to take a sip of your milk and you pick up the wrong glass without looking and it's grapefruit juice. The shock is devastating. In this case, you're all ready for a foamy lather-up and then the conditioner lands flat on your head like butterscotch syrup on a sundae.

8:19:22 A.M.: "Just put the shampoo on after the conditioner," wife says. There are a lot of things in this world that can be reversed, I tell her. But the fraternal order of shampoo and conditioner is not one of them.

8:50 A.M.: Reach in drawer for spoon for cereal. Come up with this big shoehorn-sized thing. Why the hell do we have so many spoons, all these shapes and sizes? I've got to start minimizing. From this point on I'm going with one spoon.

9:02 A.M.: Seek out wife. This is my one spoon. Where do you want me to keep it? "I don't care. Put it in your pocket," she says.

9:05 A.M.: One. That's it. I'm going to get down to one of everything. One pen, one TV, one phone, one dog, one goal in life. "You don't even have any goals," wife says. That's a good start, I say.

9:10 A.M.: Go to pick out a fork.

9:21 A.M.: Head out for work. Before getting in car I check wallet to see if my prized possession is still there. There it is, my grocery store receipt from 3/24/00 and right across the top, directly above the $1.39 mushrooms, is the proud declaration: PRESLEY WAS YOUR CASHIER TODAY.

9:22 A.M.: Hold it up to the light. It's so beautiful. Since they've been putting cashier's names on receipts I've been collecting the best ones. I almost had a SINBAD but it was a stock guy who only got on the register when it was really busy, and the one time I got lucky it turned out he was using the head cashier's drawer and I walked away with nothing but a KAREN. I was so upset I went home and kicked the second dog. But this, this Elvis one makes up for everything.

10:07 A.M.: Stop at Mobil Mart on way to office. I never buy anything, just give my ten dollars for gas and walk out, but at the last second I catch a glimpse of the cashier's name tag: KAMASUTRA.

10:08 A.M.: Aaah, give me a can of that Copenhagen snuff. He quickly rings it up and hands me the receipt. I take a few steps away and my heart sinks at the sight of THANKS FOR SHOPPING AT DALE HANRATTY'S MOBIL MART. I'm so distraught I turn back to the counter to give him the receipt to throw out for me but he misunderstands. "Fresh," he says. "Salesman just brought in Monday. Fresh." No, I'm not returning the snuff, I say. I don't want my money back. The snuff is grand. I'm returning the receipt. "No, no, fresh." But? "Manager in at two," he says.

10:31 A.M.: On way up to office run into coworker who is uncharacteristically chipper this morn. "I'm dating a security guard," he says. You can't do that, I say. People don't have relationships with security guards. It's like that other rule that you can't marry someone you met on public transportation. "No, don't you remember," he says. "The rule is women can't go out with male security guards but guys can go out with female security guards." Oh, that's right.

10:47 A.M.: New chairs have arrived. Company is trying to convince employees to get new chairs in lieu of pay increases this year. Last year, they tried to give everybody seats near the window but everybody's backs got sweaty.

11:01 A.M.: I decline a new chair but the ones with the 180-degree platform footrests are pretty sharp. "Sure you wouldn't like one of these, Terry," the boss says, spinning a burgundy model with a spider base, waterfall contour seat, and self-skinned polyurethane armrests. He's the devil.

11:18 A.M.: Two marketing guys stop in front of my desk to finish a high-powered discussion. "It's a good idea," the one guy says. "Yeah, but does he have the wherewithal to pull it off?" the other says.

11:19 A.M.: "Did they stage that?" my cubicle neighbor asks. I don't know, I say, but do you know what wherewithal is? "I don't know," he says. "But I'm sure you haven't got it."

11:19:06 A.M.: Oh, I've got wherewithal.

11:48 A.M.: Chipper colleague who sits across the room has one of those erasable boards like Venus and Serena Williams's father keeps holding up during tennis tournaments with sayings like I LOVE MY WIFE and I DRINK GOAT'S MILK. He's got it high over his head, making a bold confession: I'M DATING A SECURITY GUARD.

12:03 P.M.: Some people are accepting the new chairs and still keeping their old chairs. "For guests," they say. "How 'bout another chair?" the boss taunts me. "Two chairs are better than one." This is ridiculous, I'm on my first day of being a minimalist and people are trying to push a second chair into my cubicle. I'm ready to go no chair, chairless. I'll come into work every morning and it'll just be like moseying up to a bar. Yeah! Does anybody want my chair? I say. "I'd like three chairs," a chipper voice says. It's yours.

12:17 P.M.: For some reason I get a hankering for a butterscotch sundae.

12:22 P.M.: On my way out, erasable head is holding up board that says, I LOVE MY THREE CHAIRS.

12:24 P.M.: Go to lunch and eat alone.

12:51 P.M.: Decide at lunch that between my home life, work life, and secret life, I'm going to have to decide which one I should keep. Have to at least narrow it down to two.

12:54 P.M.: Home life? Where would I sleep? Secret life? Without that, what would I do with myself? Work life?

12:55 P.M.: That was easy.

1:11 P.M.: Vendor in lobby of building shows me a picture in a tabloid of a used-car salesman who was buried in a mummy-like fireproof suit because he knew he was going to hell. "That's just an artist's rendering," he says of the picture of the guy in the suit.

1:23 P.M.: Guy two floors up who also collects receipts and has been trying to trade for the Presley calls to titillate me. "Maybe this will titillate you," he says. "Ready? . . . Jacko." Get out! I say. Where? "In a convenience store in the sleepy little retirement community of Tamarac." Get out, there's a Jacko in Tamarac?

1:24 P.M.: Borrow colleague's erasable board to hold up an announcement: THERE'S A JACKO IN TAMARAC.

2:00 P.M.: Manager at Mobil Mart must just be getting in about now.

2:06 P.M.: "How do you decide to end it?" the boss says to me. Excuse me? I say. "These timelines, how do you decide when to stop each day? Sometimes it's eleven at night, sometimes it's three-forty-five in the afternoon, sometimes it's . . ."

2:07 P.M.: I really wasn't putting that much thought into it, I say. Sometimes it just feels right or it's the end of the workday or something profound happens or my pen runs out of ink or I have to follow some strange woman. You know, I can't ever imagine this actually happening but someday there may be no beginning, like if I sleep all day or something. "Really," he says.

3:12 P.M.: I've got keyboard on top of my terminal, which works better when standing up but my arms get in the way of screen a little. Guy in cube next to me looks up as if he looks down on me. I've got my mind set on this. I'm taking a stand, I say. "Yeah, but do you have the wherewithal to pull it off?" he says.

3:13 P.M.: Oh, I've got the wherewithal.

3:41 P.M.: Boss comes over with a catalog picture of a chair that's set for late 2000 release. It's called "The Hawk." Are those wings? I say, a bit interested. "I've got you, haven't I?" he says. "This is the chair, isn't it? Guys would give up a year's pay for this baby. Look at it. Look at it." He is definitely working for the devil. This picture of the chair is just an artist's rendering, isn't it? I say. You think I'm going to be fooled into giving up my raise by an artist's rendering? "Why not?" he says.

3:42 P.M.: Have you thought about being fitted for a fire-proof suit? I ask.

3:51 P.M.: Decide to leave. Not because my feet are starting to hurt but because I feel kind of stupid standing while everyone else is sitting.

4:01 P.M.: "Sure you don't want to sit over here in my cube for a while," says coworker with three chairs. "You could be my first guest."

4:02 P.M.: On way out Chipper sticks the erasable board in my face. On the front it says: I'D MARRY SOMEONE I MET ON A BUS. On the back it says: I'M THE KING OF THE WORLD!

4:04 P.M.: While cutting through lobby I decide it's going to be all secret life from now on. I'm undercover. Pull my one spoon out of my pocket and hold it up to check reflection and see if anyone is following behind me. Lucky for them they're not.

4:52 P.M.: Stop at store on way home to get some shampoo and conditioner in one.

4:58 P.M.: Cashier's name is: BARBARELLA.

DAY 6
It Happens

Sleep all day.

DAY 7
Time to Make the Doughnuts

*"First of all, people always think I'm kidding,
but I promise you I'm not! If there's anything
I hate it's irony."*

—MONA BEADLE

9:18 A.M.: I'm stalling.

9:19 A.M.: I'm sitting in the car, afraid to go in. For some people it's going to the dentist or public speaking or waiting on death row. For me, it's ordering a dozen doughnuts.

9:19:41 A.M.: Who eats doughnuts? I said to my wife when she handed me the Dunkin' Donuts coupon first thing this morning. "We do," she said. Oh, yeah.

9:20 A.M.: It's Sunday, so customers are five deep at the counter but they've always got plenty of help and it all happens so fast. "Next." "Next." "Next."

9:20:12 A.M.: I know it's a lack of preparation on my part. I should make a list, I should check it twice. I sometimes study the pictures in the ad but, in real life, preconceived images of doughnuts are always misleading.

9:20:34 A.M.: Instead of this stupid coupon there should be like a catalog for people who can't really handle the frenzy of making a dozen decisions, a dozen choices in a matter of seconds.

9:20:41 A.M.: Yeah, a doughnut catalog.

9:20:43 A.M.: Lady in Wendy's uniform cuts ahead of me in line.

9:20:48 A.M.: Why a dozen, anyway? After two or three it's over. You might think you'll put the box aside and have another for an afternoon snack or perhaps as dessert with dinner but that never happens They really lose their appeal by noon. Who was it that said, "Doughnut infatuation is fleeting."

9:21 A.M.: "Next."

9:21:21 A.M.: It's too soon. I like to start ordering in my head before they get to me but up until now my vision of the racks has been obscured by the clerks. The Pakistanis seem to have grown considerably since the last time I was in. I've heard Pakis get their main growth spurt in their mid-thirties but this is my first experience with what kind of havoc such a quirk can wreak on society.

9:21:32 A.M.: "I think you were first," the gentleman beside me says. No, no, you go ahead, I say. Doughnut infatuation is fleeting.

9:21:39 A.M.: He orders a plain cruller and a black coffee. He lives a life without complications. Everything is good enough for him as is. No elaboration necessary. He wouldn't have a dozen of anything, except maybe collectible Zippos. He's a simple man, content to muddle through this world without the extras, without sprinkles.

9:21:51 A.M.: "Next."

9:22 A.M.: "One of each sprinkle," I say. That always gets me off to a good start 'cause there's the multicolor sprinkle, the chocolate sprinkle, the pink sprinkle . . . before you know it you've got four in the box. "No sprinkles today," the clerk says, turning back to the rack. It's a bold turn, an "Okay, your move! You blind, indecisive unprepared jerk-off" kind of motion. What a man's man. If I was making like a testosterone doughnut I would use like four cups of him.

9:22:09 A.M.: The crowd behind me is deep and hungry for pastry, everyone is watching and waiting for me to perform. But my mind is racing. I think this is the first time in a week I haven't thought about my armpits or my ex-con roommate. The crowd goes silent. Everyone is counting on me but no one has confidence in me.

9:22:11 A.M.: All I can do is stare at those plain doughnuts. I always use them for my last choice, though. I like to say, "One plain" and then watch them tuck it into the twelfth spot. I could blurt it out now but then I lose my closer. Damn!

9:22:13 A.M.: Guy two back says, "Glazed," trying to pick for me. There's always someone who thinks they know me better than I know myself.

9:22:15 A.M.: Glazed, I say.

9:22:23 A.M.: I step it up. "Two apple cinnamon." But it's a false bravado, it's not what I want. It's just a pitiful ruse, I want the guy two back who should mean absolutely nothing to me to think I'm suddenly sure of myself.

9:22:38 A.M.: "Who does he think he's kidding?" The guy two back nudges the guy three back.

9:22:50 A.M.: To my left is a woman wearing her church best and holding an adorable baby dolled up in a plaid dress and white leggings. Lord, I wish she would pick me up in her arms like that baby, hold me, and whisper in my ear, "Coconut cream."

9:22:52 A.M.: Coconut cream, I say.

9:22:54 A.M.: "No coconut cream."

9:23 A.M.: Boston cream, I say. Boston cream. "Two?" he asks. That's not what I had in mind but at this rate it's a grand idea. Yes, I say. Yes. And a white powdered grape jelly.

9:23:06 A.M.: Where'd that come from?

9:23:09 A.M.: It's getting into that blurred territory now— Okay, that's four. No, five. No, there were no sprinkles. Is it two? Or is it six?

9:23:13 A.M.: The clerk pulls that stunt they do to deliberately taunt people, tilting the box up so you can't see how many are in there and forcing you to say something like, "Is that seven?"

9:23:23 A.M.: Is that seven?

9:23:25 A.M.: "No," he says, without providing any additional information.

9:23:38 A.M.: I know there are people who just walk in and order a dozen glazed and walk out and then put them on a counter at work and say, "Hey everybody, I brought doughnuts," and then everyone walks over and sees that it's only glazed and thinks of that person as weak and unimaginative. But I have the utmost respect for those people. You have to have an extremely strong will to surrender like that, or at the very least have someplace else to be.

9:23:48 A.M.: Just make the rest of them glazed, I say firmly.

9:23:52 A.M.: Some people say baseball is the metaphor for life, but this is it for me. The rushed decisions, the frantic pace, the time flying by, the mixed signals, everyone counting on me but no one having any confidence in me, immediate regrets, peer pressure, men from foreign lands reaching puberty in their mid-thirties, false moves, fleeting satisfaction, the ridicule, the taunting, the apprehension, and the last grasp for one's dignity.

9:24 A.M.: Wait! One plain.

DAY 8

Ripples in the Soup

"Plastics."

—CAREER ADVICE IN *THE GRADUATE*

8:18 A.M.: Give no thought to what I'm going to wear today.

8:33 A.M.: Put a lot of thought into packing my lunch.

9:20 A.M.: Lady in convenience store is complaining about getting a ticket for going through a stop sign. "When I got in the middle of the intersection I realized I ran it, so I stopped and went back. And he still gave me a ticket," she says. "I don't think you can go back for a stop sign," another customer tells her. "That would be like time traveling."

10:11 A.M.: There are sealed envelopes on everyone's desks at work. Seems after we all had lunch with the big boss, we were each graded individually on our performances. "We're getting graded on our lunch performance now?" someone squeals. "I give up."

10:15 A.M.: New guy is in shock. "I got points off for mumbling and not looking up while I was talking. What the . . . I'm sorry, I have to look at my food when I eat." His neighbor pulls it out of his hands. "Look," she laughs, "under 'other comments' it says you talked into your soup. Your head was so far down, your words were causing ripples in the soup."

10:16 A.M.: "Ripples in the soup," he shouts. "That's bull."

10:18 A.M.: Leave my envelope sealed.

10:44 A.M.: Coworker is trying to figure out what you say if you have more than one Lexus. Is it the same as if you have more than one, say, moose?

10:48 A.M.: I'm not sure exactly what the rule is on words like moose (maybe someone just has to have the nerve to decide and make it official), so we try it in a sentence. "The whole parking lot was filled with nothing but Lexus."

10:49 A.M.: "The whole parking lot was filled with nothing but Lexuses," he says.

10:49:14 A.M.: We decide: Lexus is the same as moose. It's official.

11:12 A.M.: New company policy comes down. "Since no one seems to be giving any thought to what they're wearing," it begins, "we decided to pay someone to think about it and they came up with: *Flexwear*."

11:13 A.M.: Immediately call a neighbor who just graduated from college last week. What are your plans for the future? I ask. "I'm not really sure," he says. Well, I've got one word for you, I say.

11:14 A.M.: Flexwear.

11:18 A.M.: Sales guy is laboring over his expense report. You look like that's taking every bit of concentration you have, I say. "I haven't had this much trouble focusing since I read page 191 of *Cold Mountain*," he says. When

Ada and Ruby have a hair contest? I ask. "Yeah, you been there?" I feel your loss of concentration, brother.

11:22 A.M.: Turns out Flexwear is more of a plan than a new type of clothing. Seems after Casual Fridays led to Casual Summers, things started to get out of hand so they're trying to rein it back in by changing the policy to Dress for Your Day.

11:23 A.M.: Art guy immediately reaches into desk drawer and takes out a pair of knickers.

11:24 A.M.: Memo says since everyone in the company has different demands and roles, the directors have agreed on the Flexwear concept. You should wear a suit when it's appropriate, jeans when it feels right, etc. We're to use common sense. "Employees Are to Dress for the Day Ahead of Them."

11:34 A.M.: "I'm going to ask if I can go home and change. I've got a meeting this afternoon," marketing lady says. I don't know if a person can go back and dress for the day ahead of them, I say. That would be like time traveling.

11:35 A.M.: "I live too far away to go home and change," one coworker says enviously. Me, too, I say. "I do have a soft-ball uniform in the car," he contemplates. Go for it, I say.

11:48 A.M.: "I opened you-know-who's envelope," a colleague whispers to me. "He got points off for only telling the boss things he'd want to hear."

11:48:06 A.M.: "Wait a second, I got points off for telling him things he didn't want to hear," another worker says.

12:04 P.M.: Guy in softball uniform returns. "You could have left the mitt in the car," someone balks. On the back of his jersey it says, "Pattie's Oodles of Poodles Snip 'n' Wash." What is your role with the company again? I ask.

12:18 P.M.: Decide I overthought packing my lunch so I go to Subway. Guy in front of me is holding two slices of bread. "That's my girlfriend," he says, pointing to the girl making the subs. Okay, I say. "Her boss counts the sub rolls every day so she can't give me freebies, but if I bring my own bread she can make me a big fat sandwich. They don't count the meat." I brought my lunch, I say, heading back to the car.

12:19 P.M.: Go to lunch and eat alone. Give myself a C. I've never claimed to be anything more than average, especially when it comes to lunch.

1:01 P.M.: Pass by a new upscale, trendy restaurant. That's a lot of Lexus, I say aloud.

1:08 P.M.: Run into coworker on the way into building. "It says to dress accordingly if you're out in the field. What is that? Do you ever go out in the field?" she asks me. Me, no, I've never been out in the field, I say.

2:10 P.M.: Guy that works late just got his lunch grades. "Damn," he says. "Just because I didn't put the cloth napkin on my lap. I hate those things. It's like wearing a diaper."

2:12 P.M.: Woman who went home to change comes back carrying a suitcase. "I am ready for anything," she shouts. "What are you doing?" someone says. "The Flexwear Policy doesn't even exist now. Since you went back in time all events have changed. I don't even think you work here anymore."

2:41 P.M.: Try saying, "Ripples in the soup" three times fast.

3:10 P.M.: Several other people have changed into softball uniforms. "It's what the day calls for," they say. "You wanna play?" I hate softball, I say. I'd rather have a hair contest with Ada and Ruby than play softball. "You'd lose," Oodles of Poodles says.

3:41 P.M.: Stand by window and watch coworkers play three-on-three softball.

4:15 P.M.: Decide to walk out during sixth inning.

4:17 P.M.: On way out, woman in elevator asks me if I

could please turn around. "I have to change," she says. "I was out in the field all day but now I've got a meeting with the marketers upstairs, and then we're supposed to take a client to dinner afterward and then I have to . . ."

4:18 P.M.: Turn around.

4:34 P.M.: Can't wait to get home.

5:01 P.M.: Tell wife I'm going to lie down for awhile. Before climbing into bed I put a lot of thought into taking off my clothes.

5:11 P.M.: It's not that easy when you think about it.

DAY 9

Autographs Anyone?

"The weather is here. I wish you were beautiful."

—JIMMY BUFFETT

7:54 A.M.: You know, this pen would be good for autographs, I tell my wife. Not so much for signing eight-by-ten glossies but like basketballs and stuff like pro athletes do. "Put it back," she says. "I bought them for work."

7:55 A.M.: It's a two-pack.

8:02 A.M.: Try signing basketball. It's not as easy as you'd think. I wonder if athletes have to go to special seminars for this. This is like trying to write on the moon, I tell my wife. Try it.

8:03 A.M.: "I don't have time to autograph your basketball," she says, rushing past me. Now I know how all those heartbroken kids feel when someone like a superstar athlete blows them off. Big shot! I yell after her.

8:22 A.M.: It's too late. The laundry is scattered all over the yard—up in trees, deep in brush, mixed among the mulch. It's the whites. Damn, I didn't think of it until I went to get my socks and remembered that I'd left the basket of clean clothes in the carport with the new dog—the second dog—and you just can't do that.

8:24 A.M.: Damn, I say, looking out over the landscape. A second mortgage, a second honeymoon, a second car, a second anything would be better than a second dog. I shout to my wife: Why the hell did you have to get a second dog? It's an extra dog, for God's sake. Extra dogs don't have to be bothered with the regular stuff like barking at trespassers and chasing postal workers so they have free time for crap like this.

8:31 A.M.: The extra dog has one of my socks hanging out of his mouth and leads me to the mother lode. I have to get down on my stomach and crawl under the thorn bushes like it's barbed wire in boot camp. Man, its hard enough matching up socks as it is without this.

8:33 A.M.: I'm up on my elbows stuffing underwear down my shirt and trying to make it to what looks like an entire nest made out of my sweat socks.

8:35 A.M.: I'm bleeding and clawing at the pile when it dawns on me that this . . . is my Vietnam.

8:42 A.M.: I'm coming in loaded with yesterday's wash when extra dog comes up to me with that stupid Nerf ball and I'm about to kick him when I realize that even though things are extremely hectic at the moment and I'm already late for work I still have time for an autograph.

8:43 A.M.: It's wet and full of teethmarks but, despite the circumstances, I lay down a pretty legible signature without complaining or whining. There you go, boy.

9:01 A.M.: On way out to work neighbor asks me if I know whatever happened to Roger Clinton? I have no answer for him. "I'd just like to know that he's okay," he says.

9:44 A.M.: Booths are set up in lobby of our building and people are voting. I've never seen voters before. They look something like the people I've met who get upset when they find out Chick-Fil-A is closed on Sundays.

9:49 A.M.: At work, the "How ya doin'?" guy is pacing the halls. "How ya doin'?" he says. Fine, I say. But that's never good enough for him. "How you doin'?" he says. I'm not lying to you—I swear, I tell him. But he wants more. He backs me into a corner. "How you doin'?" My knees are raw and my hands are bloody from gathering up my wash, I shout. "How you doin'?" he says. The whites, I yelp. It was the white load!

9:52 A.M.: "That's better," he says, setting me free.

10:12 A.M.: New employee gets back from an interview with Human Resources. "They asked me to describe myself in three words," he says. What'd you say? "Bold and Beautiful."

10:13 A.M.: Everyone thinks the new guy is going to work out.

10:55 A.M.: Wife calls to tell me that just before she left for work today our ex-con houseguest had been on top of our Adirondack chairs. Now, let me be sure I've got this right. He was doing some kind of high-incline push-ups atop two Adirondack chairs while wearing a knapsack full of rocks and weights on his back because otherwise it would be too easy. And that's when he slipped? Into the pool?

10:56 A.M.: "That's when he slipped. Into the pool," my wife says. "And when I ran out he was struggling at the bottom trying to wriggle out of the backpack, like one of those escape artists. Like Houdini." Like Houdini, that's cool, I say.

10:56:42 A.M.: How long was he down *there?* I ask. "It was awhile," my wife says. Do you think he suffered any brain damage?

10:57 A.M.: "How would we tell?" she says.

11:58 A.M.: Go to break room to get a bag of chips. The vendor has moved all the chips up to the top shelf in the machine so if you buy a bag of salt-and-vinegar chips it will have a three-foot drop to the bottom. "That's too far," I say to myself.

11:59 A.M.: Especially *these* chips. They're very delicate.

12:01 P.M.: Look around, trying to think what MacGyver would do.

12:04 P.M.: Can't think of what MacGyver would do, but MacGyver only had an hour show so he had to think up stuff fast. I have all day.

12:21 P.M.: There's a sweater hanging on the back of one of the break-room chairs. It's just sitting there like your third-grade teacher's did two hundred days out of the year until that one day when she said, "Oooh, I've got goose bumps," and snuggled it around her freckled shoulders.

12:22 P.M.: Try to think if I have any more fond hanging-on-the-back-of-the-chair sweater memories.

12:28 P.M.: Don't.

12:29 P.M.: Push door at bottom of vending machine open and insert the soft sweater to cushion the landing.

12:30 P.M.: Hit A4 and the bag floats down on butterfly wings and gently settles into the folds of the sky-blue sweater. I have never seen anything so beautiful.

12:36 P.M.: Go to lunch and eat alone.

1:11 P.M.: On way back from lunch I stop at music store.

There's a sports memorabilia shop in the same strip center and I look in the window and stare at a baseball that must have thirty names on it. I can't imagine. It's tough enough having to maneuver around the threads and everything on a ball that is no bigger than my fist. I can't fathom what kind of precision skills and penmanship mastery it would take to have to also be sure not to step on one of your teammates J's.

2:01 P.M.: Coworker is playing darts without the darts. He's just standing there, staring at the board from ten paces away. "Something is missing in my life," he says. Do you have a second dog? I inquire. Or how 'bout a sweater for the back of your chair?

2:19 P.M.: New guy is wearing one of those nose breather things like pro athletes do.

2:20 P.M.: Nobody thinks new guy is going to work out.

2:34 P.M.: Read news brief about a nineteen-year-old who survived an eight-story balcony fall up in Panama City yesterday. He landed on a tiki hut. What a great postcard that will make to send the folks back home. "Slipped off balcony. Eight floors. Wow. Thought of you guys on way down. Luckily landed on tiki hut bar. Cheers. Met girl named Tara. She's sweet. Anyway, the weather is here. I wish you were beautiful. See you soon, Phil."

3:01 P.M.: Take out my new "Things to Not Do" notebook the boss told me to start keeping because things didn't work out so well with the "Things to Do" organizational workbook he gave me last month. Write that it took thirty-two minutes to buy a bag of chips when it should have taken only one, but then scratch it out because I think I might be exaggerating the time.

3:18 P.M.: Ask office manager if she has anything I can sign. "Payroll," she says. No, I mean like sports equipment I can practice autographing. "I have a Frisbee in the car," she says enthusiastically. No, Frisbees are too easy.

3:54 P.M.: Call Florida Marlins main office and ask if when players make the leap from the minors to the majors they attend a special seminar on how to write on a baseball, especially when it's a really crowded baseball like when the whole team has to sign one and if so are civilians allowed to take the class.

3:55 P.M.: No and no.

4:02 P.M.: New guy lets me autograph his nose breather. I have a little trouble at the peak but it's all downhill from there and people are stopping by to check it out. "You let him autograph your nose breather?" everybody asks him. "That's cool."

4:10 P.M.: Everybody thinks the new guy is going to do just fine.

4:22 P.M.: "How ya doin'?" guy is working the hallway. The cool guy who all he ever says is "Heavy" is in his sights. "How ya doin'?" he says to him. "Heavy," the heavy guy says and slides right by.

4:23 P.M.: Decide maybe I can get past him and make it to the restroom if I have the right attitude. I've got kind of a lope going as he zooms in on me. "How ya doin'?" he says. Heavy, I say. Not so fast, his body says, cutting me off. "How ya doin'?"

4:24 P.M.: I've got an extra dog, I say.

4:24:09 P.M.: "How you doin'?" he says.

4:24:22 P.M.: There's a little space to the left so I could maybe make it to the ladies' room if I shoot the gap but even that's a long shot. He's very fast.

4:25 P.M.: "How you doin'?" I . . . I . . . Oooo I've got goose bumps, I say. "How you doin'?" I autographed a nose breather today. "How you doin'?" I don't know what it's going to take. It's like confronting a troll at the end of a bridge. I don't know what the magic words are. I've got to go to the bathroom, I say.

4:26 P.M.: "How ya doin'?" Nothing's working. It actually took me thirty-five minutes to buy the chips, I say. And I'm not exaggerating. Why would I exaggerate something like that? "How ya doin'?" I have one fond hanging-on-the-back-of-the-chair sweater memory, and that's it. "How you doin'?" I don't know what's become of Roger Clinton. Aaah . . . Frisbees are easy.

4:27 P.M.: "How ya doin'?"

DAY 10

Method Working

"Hold the chicken."

—JACK NICHOLSON IN *FIVE EASY PIECES*

8:29 A.M.: Decide to work at home today. Save all that time from commuting. Save myself from all the distractions and bull that goes on in an office.

8:30 A.M.: "It'll just be pure no-nonsense work today. A grab-the-jack-hammer-and-put-your-head-down-and-don't-look-up-until-the-job-is-done kind of workday.

8:45 A.M.: Head into my home office, which is really just a room with a folded-up cot in one corner, a birdcage for a para-keet that died weeks ago in the other and—between the two—a bookshelf with one book, *Pope of Greenwich Village,* lying face-down on it. Oh, and a computer.

8:46 A.M.: Get straight to work.

8:49 A.M.: Getting straight to work.

8:54 A.M.: Straight to work . . .

8:55 A.M.: I think there's some towels left in the dryer from last night.

8:56 A.M.: Fold some towels.

9:06 A.M.: That's the problem with trying to work in your own home, the place where you store your stuff, the place where you sleep, the place where you spend most of your time doing nothing in particular. There may be nothing worse than the distractions that can plague you in your own dwelling.

9:10 A.M.: In an office you only have two options. You can either work or act like you're working. But at home you can either work or shoot hoops, watch *Regis,* write graffiti on the bathroom mirror with eyeliner, pop some porn in the VCR, sketch fruit, clip Arby's coupons, breast-feed a baby, put on baggy pajamas and dance Ally McBeal style, make up names for your keys, roll pennies, start a debate club, mix several cereals in one bowl . . . Well, you know what I mean.

9:39 A.M.: Wonder if boss would send someone over to check on me to see if I'm really working. I'd hate to have someone peek in my windows and report back: "He was folding towels."

9:40 A.M.: But no one ever assumed I was working before when I was in the office right in front of them so what would make them think any different now?

9:41 A.M.: Still, I've got some work that absolutely must be done today. People are counting on me.

9:43 A.M.: Spin around once in desk chair for good luck.

9:43:12 A.M.: What was that?

9:44 A.M.: Hear something out front. Go down the hall and poke my head

out front door but nothing's going on. It must have just been one of the cats or something.

9:48 A.M.: But as I'm closing the front door I notice how raggedy that Winnie the Pooh flag my wife has hanging over the carport looks. It's disgraceful. The once golden honey pot is faded so yellow that now it looks more like French's mustard than honey. It's pitiful.

9:49 A.M.: But what are you gonna do? I've got work to do.

10:04 A.M.: Turn computer on. Takes a minute to warm up.

10:05 A.M.: I can't stand having that hideous thing shamefully flapping over my home for one more second.

10:07 A.M.: Get ladder and climb up on roof to take down Winnie flag. Try not to let it touch the ground on the way to the garbage can.

10:12 A.M.: Now that that's settled I can finally get down to business.

10:16 A.M.: Turn TV on. Not to watch it but just to see what's on. *Five Easy Pieces* is on the Encore channel. I've never actually seen that movie. I've only seen that classic scene they always show where Jack Nicholson is ordering in the diner and the waitress won't give him wheat toast or something because it doesn't come with the breakfast he's ordering. You know, where he has to order the chicken salad sandwich on whole wheat and then tell the waitress to hold the chicken.

10:18 A.M.: Decide to prepare a picnic lunch so it'll be all ready for when I go on a picnic lunch later. But I'm not sure what exactly goes into a picnic lunch as opposed to a regular lunch.

10:22 A.M.: More of everything, I decide.

10:23 A.M.: And real silverware.

10:39 A.M.: Head back to office. Computer seems pretty much warmed up now. Let's hit it.

10:40 A.M.: Wonder if they've gotten to the part yet where the waitress puts her hand on her hip and says, "You want me to hold the chicken?" and Nicholson sneers back and says, "Yeah. I want you to hold the chicken . . . between *your knees.*"

10:43 A.M.: Go take a peek. But they're not even in a diner. Nicholson is on the back of a Beverly Hillbillies–looking truck playing a piano as the truck heads up an interstate exit ramp.

10:45 A.M.: Back to work.

10:47 A.M.: Fold some more towels.

10:51 A.M: I miss my friends. Not from work, I don't have any friends there. I miss my friends from third grade.

11:04 A.M.: Go for gum.

11:28 A.M.: Start putting down on paper a list of things I have to get done today. I find myself using a pencil instead of a pen, which is not at all like me. I hardly ever use a pencil but I find myself instinctively tilting the point on its edge and adding little shadows beneath the words on my notes. They're really quite good. When I hold the paper up it looks like words with shadows.

11:30 A.M.: Sketch fruit.

11:47 A.M.: Check in on *Five Easy Pieces.* Nicholson is getting into a tractor-trailer that U-turns and is heading off into the horizon just as his girlfriend is searching all over the gas station for him. I think I missed the chicken part.

12:12 P.M.: Go to a picnic and eat alone.

1:31 P.M.: Decide I have to make myself think I'm at the office so I can get some work done. I have to really psyche myself into it, like a method actor would do.

1:32 P.M.: I'm method working.

1:38 P.M.: Realize I'm not really at work so I do a drop and roll and yell out loud, "SWAT team in position!"

1:41 P.M.: Try balancing twenty-five-inch television on head while at the same time reaching into my pocket for car keys.

1:44 P.M.: Start a debate club.

1:45 P.M.: Open the door on the parakeet cage even though it makes no difference now since there is no parakeet. But somehow it makes me feel more free.

1:47 P.M.: The thing about work is you can always turn it around. Even if you're productivity is at an all-time low you can just pick a moment to focus all your energy and put your heart and soul into it and turn it all around.

1:48 P.M.: It can happen any second and I've still got the whole day in front of me.

1:49 P.M.: Unfold towels.

DAY 11

Ongoing Problem

"It's all good."

—O. D. B.

8:18 A.M.: This old window screen is like a fossil. All I did was touch it and it's turning to dust. I'm just going to take it out altogether so our house will be like one of those on TV where people pop in the bedroom window all the time. Friends will stick their heads in and go, "Hey," and I will say, "Hey" back, and then they will duck in and sit on the end of my bed and we will talk about our lives.

8:19 A.M.: "We don't have friends in the yard, we have squirrels," my wife says. "Leave the screen alone."

8:22 A.M.: Take screen out.

8:23 A.M.: "Either put the screen back in or close the damn window," wife says.

8:24 A.M.: Close window.

8:37 A.M.: Wife goes to work.

8:38 A.M.: Open window.

8:46 A.M.: See neighbor in driveway. Hey, I say, my bedroom window is wide open if you want to pop in tonight and talk about our lives.

8:47 A.M.: "Lucky landings," he says, which is all he's been saying to me since he saw Robbie Knievel jump thirty limos in Vegas. Apparently, that's what Robbie Knievel always says— "Lucky landings."

8:50 A.M.: I wish I had something cool to say when people say stuff to me that doesn't really deserve a response.

9:14 A.M.: On interstate on my commute to work and I'm getting upset. As I often do when I'm on the road, I get frustrated that everyone seems to be skillful with chopsticks but me. At first it was just lawyers on TV but now it seems like everyone—paramedics, orderlies, criminals—has mastered the chops.

9:34 A.M.: Rapper Ol' Dirty Bastard is on the radio. "It's all good," he says.

9:44 A.M.: While driving I practice using two Papermate pens as chopsticks. Try picking up cassettes and nickels off passenger seat but my hands are shaking as if I'm playing Operation and constantly getting buzzed.

10:08 A.M.: In parking garage a guy says to me: "If you park on the incline all your car's fluids are going to go to one side and sit there all day."

10:09 A.M.: It's all good, I say.

10:22 A.M.: Memo goes out about staff learning Spanish so we can talk to people when we go out into the field to work and not just in the hallways and stuff. Free classes are going to be offered. "Whaddayathink? You wanna do it?" a coworker asks. I've got to learn how to use chopsticks first, I say.

10:41 A.M.: Decide I'm not going to answer people who don't always address me by name, the way characters on TV always do. Even if I'm the only one in the room I want to be notified that it's me they're talking to.

10:43 A.M.: Notify everyone of my new rule. "Okay . . . Terry," they say.

11:12 A.M.: People are congregating by my cubicle. They're discussing an ongoing problem. "It's ongoing," someone says. This would be the perfect moment for me to reach into the bottom drawer of my desk like they do on TV and pull out a whiskey decanter and four glasses and say, Pull up a chair and let's see if we can't hammer this out. I'm sure we could if everyone could just sit and relax at my desk and drink whiskey without everyone thinking it's a big deal or something.

12:04 P.M.: I'm in the men's room when I hear one other person walk in. "So, Terry, what do you think about the ongoing problem?" I'm not sure (look over shoulder), Dave. "Well, let me know when you're sure, Terry." Okay, Dave.

12:18 P.M.: Go to lunch and eat alone.

12:41 P.M.: See homeless guy picking through garbage with chopsticks.

1:02 P.M.: Stop at liquor store to pick up a decanter of whiskey and four nice glasses. "Decanter? How 'bout a bottle?" the clerk says. A bottle's good.

1:21 P.M.: When I get back from lunch there are potted plants wrapped in paper on everyone's desks. Card says: "Here's a plant." And it's signed by the company. A nice metaphor for our growing business.

1:23 P.M.: For the first time, I can understand how people leave newborn babies in Dumpsters. I'm not ready for the responsibility of taking care of a plant. Unlike my situation with this company, if I don't put forth some effort it's going to die.

1:41 P.M.: Check out the Top 10 charts. "The Nookie" is number 2.

2:02 P.M.: If I leave a plant in a Dumpster it's not like anyone is going to hear its cries for help. It'll just lie there and get smothered by vats of kitchen grease, watermelon rinds, and real babies.

3:10 P.M.: People are congregating at my cubicle again. Someone has an idea that could lead to a solution to the ongoing problem but they're not married to it. "I think I've come up with a good idea but I'm not married to it," someone says. This is my window of opportunity. I lean down and reach back into the bottom drawer of my desk. I get into a bit of a struggle because I want to have the bottle in one hand and all four glasses in the other so I can bring it all up in one swoosh, but glass number 3 keeps slipping. Wait, here we go, here we go . . . Everybody pull up a chair and let's see if we can't ham . . .

3:11 P.M.: Everybody's gone.

3:12 P.M.: I quickly struggle to get the stash back into the drawer when I hear a voice behind me, "What's the racket all about, Terry?" Nothing (look over shoulder), Dave. "What is that, Terry, is that a bottle of whiskey in your desk?" Keep it down, will you, Dave? "Hey, everybody, Terry is hiding whiskey in his . . . " Hey, I'm not hiding anything. It's for everybody, like on TV when everyone has a drink in the judge's chambers, Dave. "You're not a judge, Terry." I know I'm not,

Dave. Why don't you sit down, let's see if we can't hammer this out . . .

3:14 P.M.: Maybe if I'd used a fancy decanter people would have understood it was just a metaphor for good spirits in the face of adversity and the boss wouldn't want to see me in the office.

3:15 P.M.: "I just don't want this bottle of whiskey in your desk to become an ongoing problem, Terry."

4:12 P.M.: The plant makes good camouflage when leaving early. "What are you doing with that plant, Terry?" someone asks. I'm pollinating it, I say.

4:14 P.M.: I am so sick of hearing my own name.

4:15 P.M.: Take elevator up to corporate floor I've never been on. Nice doors.

4:21 P.M.: Leave plant in front of door that says: J. B. & J. B., D. D. C. C. H., K. D. Sounds like it would make a loving and caring home.

4:22 P.M.: Not sure if I've done the right thing. Hope I don't hate myself in twenty years.

5:51 P.M.: Get home. Wife is at front door. "Come in and tell me if you notice anything different," she says. "Like that we now have four dogs and six cats." I recognize about half of them, I say. "Why don't we take a walk back to that screenless window and sit down and talk about our lives," she says.

5:52 P.M.: It's all bad.

Day 12

Paper-Bagging It

"I don't mind that I don't have a mind."

—Kurt Cobain

7:54 A.M.: Wake up from dream about taking recycling bins out to curb. This is no good, dreams are supposed to be deep and complicated so your mind can work out all your inner problems while you're sleeping, instead of in the daytime when you have to drive and try to act normal at work and stuff.

7:56 A.M.: "Maybe there was something different and intriguing in the bin," says my wife, the optimist. "A bottle with a message in it or something." Nope. I checked.

9:38 A.M.: On the fourth level of the parking garage a bunch of white guys who watched some documentary or something last night are gathered around talking about slavery.

Isn't that how it all started?

10:10 A.M.: A coworker, whose health regimen includes working out with weights every two years, is in pain. "I'm so sore I can't even shrug," he says. The only thing he had going for him was his indifference toward just about everything in life. "And now I can't even show that off," he says.

10:12 A.M.: Test: Hey, would you rather die in your sleep or in a hail of gunfire? I ask the shrugger. And you can see he's digging deep, trying to fight the pain. He always gets to flaunt his indifference to life but this is a rare opportunity to show his indifference to death and he doesn't want to pass it up. But the pain of shrugging must be unbearable. He's grimacing and his eyes are watering. His chest is trembling.

10:13 A.M.: He faints.

10:51 A.M.: Cousin calls. He's furious. "My wife is counting my beers," he yells. "Last night, while we're having our usual argument, out of the blue she says, 'Please, I'd rather not discuss it after you've had seven beers.'" Whoa, I say, were you doing one of those things where you like line the empties up in front of you? "No, that I could understand," he says. "But she just knew. I can't live like this." How many beers have you had this morning? I ask. "Hold on," he says. "I'll ask my wife."

11:18 A.M.: There's a meeting going on down the hall and we keep hearing bursts of howling laughter. None of us can remember laughing that hard except maybe the first time we saw *Take the Money and Run.* We decide the humor bar is lowered to about bootie-sock level during meetings. Getting a laugh in a meeting is akin to getting a laugh at a Republican rally by making a Clinton joke. "Or something like that," someone says.

11:54 A.M.: Cousin calls back with a long diatribe. "Count how many times I've put thirty dollars worth of gas in a twenty dollar car. Count how many Saturdays I've worked overtime in the past two years. Count how many times I've listened to her mother tell me to be sure I always have a shirt on when we visit her retirement complex. Count how many vacations I haven't taken in the past decade. Count how many good years I've got left before I've got nothin' but bad years but don't, goddamn it, be countin' my beers." Right on, I say.

12:20 P.M.: Shrugger's buddies are checking with him about lunch. "Whaddayathink, pizza or the sub place?" He looks at me, looks at them. Do you want me to do it for you? I ask. 'Cause I can do it. He's getting angry, like "I don't need anybody to shrug for me, you son of a . . ." He cringes, goes for the release button on his chair, and drops himself about a foot. The backlash causes his shoulders to bounce up slightly but it's the most pitiful, poorly executed simulated shrug anyone has ever seen. People are laughing.

12:21 P.M.: He's crying.

12:38 P.M.: Go to lunch and eat alone.

1:44 P.M.: Back in office a coworker has everyone circled up and saying, "Wait till you hear this one. It's a riot."

1:45 P.M.: She's done. Nobody laughs. "You don't think that's funny?" she shouts. "I bet if I told it in a meeting you jerks would have been howling like dingoes in heat."

3:12 P.M.: Woman is going desk to desk to notify one and all that the new office supplies are in. She's talking low, and one worker, who can't make out what she's saying, keeps asking, "What? What?" making her repeat herself. "What? What? Oh, office supplies. I thought you were saying, 'Elvis supplies.'"

3:13 P.M.: Grab pillow case I keep in my desk and scurry over to search the supply closet just in case it was me that was hearing wrong.

4:12 P.M.: Message on phone mail: "I never do it but I'm stopping at the convenience store on the way home today and getting a 16-ounce Bud with the little paper bag and everything. Her count's going to be one short before she even knows what hit her."

4:15 P.M.: Head out. Stop at convenience store. Don't really feel like a beer but do feel like using one of those little bags. Buy ginger ale. Take bag.

4:22 P.M.: Think about asking my wife for a divorce tonight but just remembered it's Friday and if I bring something like that up it might ruin the whole weekend.

4:22:12 P.M.: It can wait.

5:10 P.M.: Stop at Toys R Us to see about getting a Nintendo game for nephew. Up front, where they have game systems set up for kids to check out, there's a salesman-looking guy with a briefcase talking to the kids. He starts opening his attaché so I linger, maybe he's got some game coupons or something.

5:12 P.M.: He's a Mormon.

5:13 P.M.: New campaign must be targeting kids because his pamphlet says, "Mormons Rule." He's zeroing in on one of the older boys, about thirteen, and I wonder if I should get the manager. But then I notice that every time the Mormon salesman says something to the kid he just shrugs and I realize there's no need to worry. As long as he has the shrug down and stays in good enough shape to keep it in working order, nothing in this world can touch him.

6:12 P.M.: When I get home there's a long message on answering machine. Condensed version: "And when I go to walk the dog I'm gonna have a beer in each sock and you know I hate to litter but God save me I'm gonna unload the empties in this field at the end of my block and then I'm gonna come home and drink like half a beer and leave it on the kitchen table and say I'm going out to see the planet alignment or whatever the hell it is. And then, while Li'l Miss Calculator's staring at a half-full beer can, I'll be drinking two more in the moonlight. As long as this weather stays cool I can keep beers stashed all over the yard."

7:15 P.M.: Watch *Inside the Actor's Studio* on the Bravo Channel. It's become like my *Wheel of Fortune*. I have to watch it every night. Jessica Lange is on and says she is basically a sad person. I like her more now.

10:40 P.M.: Before going to bed, reread the John Cheever short story where the guy decides he can swim home using all his neighbors' pools. Not because I really feel like reading it but just to add to the dream stew I've got cooking.

11:02 P.M.: Figure I've got a good day's worth of raw material to work with dreamwise: Mormon salesman, Elvis supplies, the shrug-challenged, slavery—plus swimming, permanent sadness, and beer. Put marker in book and close my eyes.

11:03 P.M.: Try counting sheep.

11:06 P.M.: Try counting beers.

11:17 P.M.: Feeling woozy with all these ideas spinning in my head. As soon as I conk out I'm going to be entering a Freudian minefield, a surreal Dalí landscape.

2:12 A.M.: Xeriscape. Wake up from dream about putting bookmarker in Cheever paperback. Even the same damned spot—page 725.

2:13 A.M.: Get up to go to go the bathroom.

2:15 A.M.: Go back to bed and dream about getting up to go to the bathroom.

DAY 13

Regal Mike and Disco James

"What the dilly-O?"

—BUSTA RHYMES

8:10 A.M.: I'm going to ride this guy today, I tell my wife. I've never ridden anyone before but this guy needs riding. He needs to get a job, he needs to act civilized.

8:11 A.M.: "He's civilized," my wife says. He never even wears a shirt! I say. "Maybe he just likes to show off his tattoos," my wife says. Well, I wish he'd get a tattoo of a shirt, I say.

9:14 A.M.: He's got toothpaste on his face. What the . . . ? Honey, that's where all the toothpaste has been going. He's wearing it.

9:15 A.M.: Both cheeks are covered with about an inch of Crest Tartar Control and he's looking at me like, What the dilly-O? "It's for my acne," he says. "Toothpaste pulls the grease out." Where did you learn that, I ask, McDonald's or prison?

9:16 A.M.: "Stop riding him," my wife says.

9:20 A.M.: We have to have a family meeting, I say. It's coming to a head, whatever that means, I say.

9:25 A.M.: Take my wife aside and tell her we have to stop babying him. He's been here for over a week and I don't even think he's been to one job interview. "Don't be too rough on him. He didn't have a childhood," my wife says. "It's so sad, he told me last night he can't even picture Disney World."

9:26 A.M.: Can he picture working? I ask.

9:48 A.M.: He tells me he's got a lead on a car detailing job and wants to know if he can borrow my bicycle to go to the interview. Up to this point he's been using my wife's girlie bike. No, I say. I'll tell you when you're ready for a man's bike.

10:12 A.M.: Sit by front window and watch him ride off shirtless on a girlie bike. Makes me feel good about myself.

11:50 A.M.: Comes back from car detailing interview. Well? "Didn't go well. Didn't pass the test," he says. *They have a car detailing test?*

11:52 A.M.: "Only got one wrong," he says. A car detailing test and you get one wrong and you fail? "That's kind of tough," my wife says. "What was the question?"

11:53 A.M.: "What would you do if you found change in the cushions of the backseat . . ."

11:53:04 A.M.: "Oh, *that* kind of test," my wife and I say in unison.

11:55 A.M.: "I was just being honest," he says. "Yeah, he was just being honest," my wife says.

12:04 P.M.: Insurance company calls to readjust our home value because of recent storms. They want to know—room by room—what value we put on our possessions. Are the rates different if you invite criminals to live with you? I ask the adjuster.

12:05 P.M.: Wife kicks me. I'm just being honest, I say.

12:41 P.M.: Forced to eat alone while my wife takes ex-con boy out to lunch to console him.

1:22 P.M.: Get call for our house guest. "Tell him Regal Mike called," the voice says. Seems like all the buddies from the car-theft ring have cute little nicknames. Hence, Regal Mike because he always stole Buick Regals. My favorite is Disco James because he would always pick the cars that would start flashing all kinds of security lights once he got inside the car and he'd be in there nervously jumping around while trying to hotwire and it would look like he was dancing in disco lights.

1:30 P.M.: Sit by window and stew about this predicament. Twenty-two years old, no car, no job, no shirt—he must have some serious character deficiencies. What was that movie with Michael Keaton where he moved in and then wouldn't move out and then when he finally did decide to leave he took everything, even those little springy things that keep doors from hitting the walls. What do you call them?

1:38 P.M.: Start reading *Cold Mountain* but then get bored.

1:41 P.M.: Stick *Cold Mountain* under one end of couch and do twenty sit-ups.

1:50 P.M.: They're back.

1:51 P.M.: Regal Mike called, I say.

1:52 P.M.: "Guess who got a job?" my wife says. Get out, I say. "Starts at dawn tomorrow." Where?

1:53 P.M.: McDonald's.

1:55 P.M.: I thought he got fired from McDonald's. "Doesn't matter. He can start fresh at this location. Every McDonald's is an island unto itself. That's what the assistant manager told us."

1:56 P.M.: Okay, and they give you shirts to wear, right?

1:56:16 P.M.: "Stop riding me," he says.

2:12 P.M.: Wife decides we should all go out to dinner tonight to celebrate his new job. I decide to take a nap.

7:15 P.M.: At dinner I ask him what position he had at the other McDonald's he worked at. "Window," he says. And this makes me reevaluate everything. I may have been selling this guy short. I've often thought about how I would never be able to handle the drive-through, what with the taking orders in one ear and making change with my hands at the same time and trying to keep track of . . .

7:16 P.M.: "Not that window," he says. "The one where you just hand them the bag." Oh, that window.

10:54 P.M.: But this is good, I tell myself as I get ready for bed. I will sleep soundly tonight knowing that this twenty-two-year-old wheelless, shirtless, ex-con roomie of ours will soon be getting a weekly paycheck, and each day will take us one step closer to him getting the hell out. Suddenly, the little bit of toothpaste behind his right ear seems to give him character. I go to his room, pat him on the back and tell him in a fatherly tone, Tomorrow . . . you will go to work on a man's bike.

DAY 14

The Phone Call

"Sunday morning coming down."

—KRIS KRISTOFFERSON

8:47 A.M.: It's Sunday. I'm sleeping in. The phone is ringing like crazy. I check the Caller ID. It's McDonald's. What does he need, lunch money? Don't they give the workers free food?

8:47:04 A.M.: It's not him. It's the manager. Wants to know why he didn't show up for work at 6:45 this morning. Hold on. I'll get him, I say.

8:48 A.M.: Wake him up. He starts moaning and reaches over to pick up the phone. I run to listen in on the other line.

8:48:34 A.M.: The manager is trying to talk but all he's doing is moaning. "Do you know what time it is?" she says. "Do you know you were supposed to be here two hours ago?"

8:49 A.M.: He's just mumbling back incoherently as if he's in the middle of a dream and then says, clear as day, "Why do you guys have to open so goddamned early?"

8:49:01 A.M.: Honey, I think we've had a setback.

DAY 15

ZAP! ZOWIE!!

"Slow like honey, heavy with mood."

—FIONA APPLE

7:58 A.M.: You know, I tell my wife, I should be making biscuits from scratch, I should be spraying flexstone on old napkin holders so I can sell them out of my garage on weekends, I should be pricing one of those invisible fences that shocks the hell out of the dog when he steps off the property, I should be selling hot cocoa and nickel bags off my front stoop. I should . . . I should be doing anything but this.

7:58:51 A.M.: I shouldn't be filling out papers that are headlined: "Telecommunications Bureau Inmate Telephone System Restriction Request."

7:59 A.M.: At breakfast! At breakfast no less. "They say," my wife continues, "we have to send a current telephone bill to . . ."

8:00 A.M.: At the kitchen table, no less. In the room where I slop up my yolk with a scrap of toast, where I microwave my Ham and Cheese Hot Pockets. *In the room . . . where I bring . . . my noodles to a boil.*

8:01 A.M.: "We're never going to get this done if you don't shut up," my wife says. "I have to get to work." I don't want to get it done, I say. I don't want to know that due to my kindness we have a jobless ex-con living in our house who now has other convicts calling us from their cells in the middle of the night and the sheriff's department has to send me a special form to block inmates from calling me collect and now I'm doing prison paperwork when I should be slopping up yolk and flexstoning old napkin holders. "I don't think they actually have phones in their cells," my wife says.

8:04 A.M.: "Okay, were we getting harassing, annoying, or threatening phone calls?" she reads off the form.

8:04:48 A.M.: You know, I say, our ex-con houseguest is never going to leave. He's never going to get another job. How many times do I have to tell you, once McDonald's fires you nobody's going to touch you. That's the end of the line. I told him the other day that if he was half a man he'd just walk out of our lives, just take it down the road, and even that didn't work. "What'd he say?" He just looked puzzled and said, "Would I have legs?"

8:05 A.M.: Check number two—annoying.

9:38 A.M.: On drive to work think about what a schmucko I am for having a criminal live in my house. How much of a man am I? Two-thirds? Seven-tenths?

10:02 A.M.: While waiting at traffic light on 1-95 exit ramp, I envision that I am on a TV show and my creators are spending the long summer days trying to come up with a new story line. They are struggling.

10:10 A.M.: Guy in parking garage is laboring at backing his car in. "At the end of the day I like to shoot straight out," he says. "I do the same thing at home. I have a long driveway and I feel like Batman when I shoot out in the morning. Zap! Zowie!" I feel like half a man when I leave in the morning, I say.

10:11 A.M.: Ask security guard how much of a man he thinks I might be. "Is this like guessing someone's age at a carnival?" he says. Yeah, okay, I say.

10:12 A.M.: Starts circling me and ah-humming a lot. "Ah-hummm," he says twice on his third lap.

10:15 A.M.: Come on, you're not fitting me for a prom tux, just tell me. "Okay, okay. I used to be a chef so let me put it this way," he says. "If I was cooking up a man stew I'd only use about a teaspoon of you."

10:37 A.M.: Everyone in office is listening to coworker go on about how the friend of hers who went in for liposuction over the weekend was on the table until after midnight. "That's getting awfully close to Frankenstein territory," someone says. "Was there a thunderstorm that night?"

10:41 A.M.: Guy who always butts in butts in. "Where does all the fat go?" he says. "If he's doing lipos all night that's a lot of fat he has to get rid of."

10:41:12 A.M.: "Yeah, that's a lot of fat," everybody agrees.

10:41:23 A.M.: "You know he's not paying a biohazard company to haul off that kind of quantity of fat," he continues. "No, he's putting it in the trunk of his car and dumping half of it himself. Hefty bags of fat. It's eventually going to end up in the water system," he says. "One glass of water will be equal to eating two Big Macs. I don't want to start a fat scare but if he's dumping it we should tell somebody."

10:42 A.M.: Boss comes by and wants to know what's up. Butty here's trying to start a fat scare, I tell him. "Knock it off, Butty," he says.

10:48 A.M.: Boss stops by my desk to ask me if something's the matter. "Are you getting enough sleep at night?" No, I say, but I'm working on that. I filled out the Telecommunications Bureau Inmate Telephone System

Restriction Request form this morning. "Okay," he says, patting me fondly on the back.

11:02 A.M.: Ask Butty how much man he thinks I'm made of. "You know how they always say humans are made up of like 93 percent water?" he says. Yeah. "Well, you're 100 percent. No man. All water. Got it?"

11:15 A.M.: Got it.

11:41 A.M.: Cousin calls to let me know that as of Friday night he is Prozac-free. Switching to Zoloft? "No, *nada*," he says. "My doctor is taking me off everything. I can't wait to be in a bad mood. I'm going to make a three-day weekend out of it."

12:09 P.M.: Go to lunch and eat two Big Macs alone.

12:51 P.M.: Stop to fill out form to close my checking account at bank. "Can I ask you why you're closing it?" the clerk says. I don't like the new name, Washington Mutual, I tell her. I liked Great Western. I liked that a lot. "But we're going to have much better services than before," she says. That's not important, I say.

12:56 P.M.: Very detailed form. "Sorry there's so much paperwork," clerk says. Nonsense, I say. As long as I'm not filling out papers to keep convicts from calling my house I love bureaucracy. It's all good.

1:19 P.M.: Boss is sitting in my chair when I get back from lunch. "What do you see in your future here, Terry?" Future? I don't know about the future, I say. But I'm looking forward to next season. I think my creators might come up with a new story line.

2:12 P.M.: Wife calls. "They have a spot on the form for exceptions and I'm going to make an exception for Ronald," she says. "He says he'll only call on holidays." What is this, the pick-our-favorite-inmates-home-phone game? I shout. Don't go soft on me now. I'm not giving in on this. I want to be able to look myself in the mirror and say, My phones are convict-free. We can stay on the line for an hour arguing about it but I will never give in, I tell her. You have no idea what I'm made of.

3:12 P.M.: Head into the restroom. Look in mirror and say: My phones are convict-free, except on holidays.

3:13 P.M.: Pass Butty on way out of restroom. "What the heck were you doing in there?" he says. What? I say. "That's the men's room." He grins.

3:21 P.M.: Browse Bed Bath & Beyond grand opening sale catalog. There's a big center spread with all kinds of picnicware. I thought I went on a picnic last week but I couldn't have. I didn't have half the equipment necessary for a real picnic. Try to add up what the initial investment would be.

3:24 P.M.: I can't afford to picnic.

4:01 P.M.: Get in elevator to ride down to break room. Woman in elevator compliments the guy by the buttons on his tattoo. "I like the way it jumps out at you," she says. "Thanks," he says. "You have any tattoos?" "Yeah," she says. "You want to see it?" And before you can say Zip! Zowie! she's opening the front of her pants and pulling down the back for all to see what looks like a bouquet of cellophane-wrapped grocery store flowers at the base of her spine. "That's nice," button man says.

4:02 P.M.: She gets off elevator and button man says to me: "Always ask a woman if she has a tattoo. They love to show them and you never know where they're gonna be. And that's the best advice I'm ever gonna give you." You're all man, aren't you? I say. Can I get your card? "Sure," he says.

4:12 P.M.: Keep staring at vending machine in break room. "Are you looking for something in particular?" the irritated guy behind me says. Toast scraps, I say, walking away. That's all that's left for me in life now. Toast scraps.

4:17 P.M.: An old associate passes me on way back to office. "What's up with you?" she says. Can't afford to picnic, I say.

4:21 P.M.: Boss is standing by my desk with tall Argentinean-looking woman. "I want you to meet someone," he says. Hi, I say. Do you have any tattoos? "Nuuu," she says. I like the way you say *no,* I say. "Come on, I want you to meet someone else," the boss says to her.

4:44 P.M.: Figure if I was hanging out with a tall Argentinean woman I wouldn't be paying attention to whether my employees were sneaking out early or not so I book.

4:48 P.M.: During commute I picture the writers arguing over my new story line. Several people want me to have an angel, several don't.

5:15 P.M.: I don't know who to side with.

5:41 P.M.: When I get home I decide to back into driveway so nose of car is pointed out. Today, schmucko. Tomorrow, Batman.

Day 16

General Malaise

"Ain't there nothin' I can take?"

—Harry Nilsson

7:35 A.M.: Get up early to call in sick to work. Don't want to take the chance that I'll feel better in an hour and decide to go in.

7:40 A.M.: Go back to bed.

9:01 A.M.: I'm glad I called in sick because now I get to stay home.

9:02 A.M.: But I feel like crap.

9:15 A.M.: Contemplate calling the doctor, but then what? Then I'd have to go to the doctor. People keep telling me, "Whatever you do, don't ever go to a doctor. They will find something wrong. Your urine will be cloudy, an odd mole will appear on your back, your heart will be enlarged, something will be growing somewhere. You will not make it to the holidays."

10:01 A.M.: Drink some water but it doesn't agree with me.

10:02 A.M.: Call wife to tell her water doesn't agree with me. "You should go to the doctor," she says.

10:15 A.M.: Look up doctor's number and write it on erasable board on fridge so it's there when I'm ready.

10:16 A.M.: Would it really be so bad not to make it to the holidays this year?

10:41 A.M.: Watch TV commercial advertising a video of greatest hits from Dean Martin roasts. Contains lots of Totie Fields bonus footage if ordered today.

10:44 A.M.: Erase doctor's number and replace with 1-800 number for roast tape.

11:04 A.M.: Go to store for ginger ale. On way I press number 4 to change radio station. Nothing happens. I obviously didn't apply enough pressure on the button. My God, my strength is so depleted I can no longer have an impact on my car radio.

11:21 A.M.: Maybe the ginger ale will help.

11:22 A.M.: Tastes like water.

11:28 A.M.: Call wife to tell her that even ginger ale doesn't agree with me. "You should go to the doctor," she says.

11:31 A.M.: Go to computer and put Mayo Clinic health CD in. Try to look up the "Just One of Those Things Going Around" section because that's what I'd like this to be, but it doesn't seem to exist.

11:41 A.M.: I have a burning and tightening in my chest so I look up heart problems just so I can eliminate that.

11:42 A.M.: I'm having a heart attack. I've got the light headedness, chest discomfort, and mostly I've got . . . general malaise.

11:44 A.M.: Wait. Every health problem in here lists general malaise. I've got everything.

11:45 A.M.: Call doctor. I'm just going to make it worse in my own mind if I don't get checked out.

11:46 A.M.: "We don't have any openings today," the receptionist says. "Are you ill?" Yes, I say, explaining my symptoms.

11:47 A.M.: "General what?"

11:47:14 A.M.: Malaise.

11:48 A.M.: "Okay, the doctor will call you back shortly," she says.

12:03 P.M.: Watch biography on Bobby Darrin. In an old film clip Darrin says he can't stop snapping his fingers no matter what. It's uncontrollable.

12:04 P.M.: Wonder if I have the strength to snap.

12:20 P.M.: Clap instead.

12:26 P.M.: Try to eat lunch alone. Take a sip of ginger ale and stare at pictures of food in holiday magazines.

1:04 P.M.: Drawn back to computer and the Mayo Clinic. Look at different heart problems. One is called atrial fibrillation and flutter. A flutter wouldn't be so bad. My heart's aflutter.

1:05 P.M.: This "heart skips a beat" one doesn't sound so terrible either.

1:07 P.M.: Start to give myself a self-examination but seems kind of perverted so I do it again.

1:09 P.M.: Wife calls and I tell her I'm doing a self-examination. "You better see a doctor," she says. I am, I say. They're all booked up, but once the doctor hears my symptoms I'm sure they'll squeeze me in. Oh, and my armpits feel fat all of the sudden. Did I tell you that before? "No," she says. "You must have forgot."

1:18 P.M.: On E! channel I watch a reenactment of Rita Hayworth's father trying to teach the young Rita to dance by belittling and ridiculing her. The narrator says it was traumatic for the child but all they show in the dramatization is dancing feet so it takes some of the sting out of it.

1:28 P.M.: Call work to tell them I think I've got general malaise. "That's what we've suspected all along," they say.

2:04 P.M.: Doctor calls. Wants to know exactly how I feel. I start with the burning and tightening in the chest. And when I stand up I feel lightheaded and when I sit down I feel queasy. "Well, it doesn't sound like an emergency to me," he says. *Doesn't sound like an emergency?* I'm reading the symptoms for a heart attack verbatim from the Mayo Clinic CD. "So," the doctor says, "why don't we make an appointment for about two weeks from now when we have an opening and we'll do a complete physi—"

2:05 P.M.: And general malaise, I say, trying to get his attention . . .

2:05:23 P.M.: Oh, and chubby armpits.

2:05:30 P.M.: "Chubby what?"

2:06 P.M.: If I could just get some antibiotics, I say. Just in case something is hiding in me, something deep down and dormant. "I don't think antibiotics would help with what you've got there," he says. But what have I got? "Hard to say. We'll see you on the seventeenth."

2:07 P.M.: Wait. Water doesn't agree with me. I no longer have an impact on my car radio . . .

2:08 P.M.: After I hang up a couple of minutes after he did I wonder what the use of the family doctor is in these modern times. He tells me I can't see him because it's not an emergency. If it was an emergency I wouldn't have even called him—I'd have gone to the emergency room. For the regular stuff you go see your doctor. If I can't come in for the regular stuff then what are doctors doing? Have family doctors taken themselves out of the picture except for perhaps yearly physicals and shots for school kids?

Who plans their illnesses two weeks ahead?

2:10 P.M.: Call wife to tell her the doctor refused to see me. "Did you mention the general malaise?" she asks. Acted like he hears it a thousand times a day, I say.

2:15 P.M.: Feel much better now that the doctor won't see me.

2:22 P.M.: Go back to Mayo Clinic and read about kidneys, just for the heck of it.

2:31 P.M.: Sneeze.

2:31:17 P.M.: That's good. Something's going out.

2:34 P.M.: I know where this is headed. A couple of days before the seventeenth I'm going to feel 400 percent better, but then they're going to get me in for all those tests, all that bending over and doesn't that urine look a little cloudy and have you always had that mole on your back and there seems to be some enlargement of the heart here and . . .

2:35 P.M.: Call to cancel doctor's appointment.

Riding the Curve

"My life is good."

—RANDY NEWMAN

7:53 A.M.: I just realized nothing is great anymore. Nothing we do or say. Not movies or food or literature or music, nothing. The most we can expect something to be is good, so we've begun grading things on the curve to make them great.

8:25 A.M.: Traffic is jamming up. Fall in love with woman driving the green Honda Del Sol behind me.

8:26 A.M.: It doesn't last.

9:12 A.M.: Turn on car radio. Chris Rock is on the Howard Stern show. "You are the funniest man in America, the greatest," Howard tells him. "But it's a weak market right now," says Rock, who's obviously aware of the new grading system.

9:14 A.M.: There's the woman in the Del Sol again. I don't know what I ever saw in her.

9:35 A.M.: Boss is standing at my desk. Wants my United Way contribution. Now! In cash.

9:44 A.M.: Trying to chart it out. If great is good then good is okay and okay is tolerable and . . .

9:45 A.M.: "How you doin' today?" a coworker asks. Fine, I say, which, according to the curve, means I have one, maybe two reasons for living and I'm looking for them right now so could you please get out of my light.

9:50 A.M.: Cousin calls to tell me he's going for his yearly physical. Anything bothering you? I ask. "No, feeling pretty good," he says. Then would you mind telling the doctor your armpits feel fat? I ask.

9:51 A.M.: "What?" he says. I thought I was having a heart attack but now I feel fine except my armpits are still heavy, I inform him. It feels like I've got little water balloons under each pit but I really don't want to tell the doctor that. "Oh, right. But it's okay if I do it," he says. Things like that come easier to you, I say. "That's true," he says.

10:37 A.M.: Get e-mail from someone who says they're going to send me a message in Sinatraspeak. Seems you write a regular message then send it to the Sinatra web site and then they Sinatrasize it and send it on as Frank e-mail. "It's going to take a little time, though," the message says. "First you have to sign something that says you won't hold them liable if some woman gets insulted by being called a broad or something."

11:47 A.M.: I keep a list in my desk of things I want to do before I die and I just thought of another one. I want to be the guy who starts the impromptu clapping. You know the guy: He's usually in the back of the room and someone has just said or done something worthy of applause. It's not the type of setting where one would start clapping but one secure individual takes it upon his- or herself to put his or her hands together into a slow, hard clap that gradually builds until monstrous applause erupts throughout the room. God, I want to be that guy.

12:22 P.M.: Go to lunch and eat alone.

1:18 P.M.: On way back from lunch I have this unnerving vision. I'm at the back of a jam-packed room. My hands are meeting in a glorious *clap! clap! clap!* . . . and not one soul in the entire room is joining in. I'm just one asshole clapping. I'm the lone clapper.

2:12 P.M.: Cousin calls back. Tells me that when he told the doctor about my problem and he couldn't find anything he had like half the staff in the office come in to take a look. "I had to stand in front of everybody with both my arms up in the air," he says. "It was like a medical stickup."

2:13 P.M.: Well? I say. "No one saw water balloons under there." Yeah, but he must have given you some advice, some medication you might want to try. "His voice got real low and he said, 'Ignore your armpits.' "

2:14 P.M.: *Just ignore them?* I immediately realize I will never be able to get anything done for the rest of my life because ignoring my armpits will now encompass all of my thoughts and energy. People will be able to walk up to me during any waking hour and ask me what I'm doing and my answer will always be: "Ignoring my armpits."

3:42 P.M.: Special alert: Hit man–looking guy I've never seen before comes into office. Someone tells me he's our main boss. He hustles the entire staff into one of the offices for some big announcement. "Did we win a prize?" someone says.

3:43 P.M.: He breaks the news that our everyday boss has left to go find himself, kind of like Albert Brooks in *Lost in America.* He rambles on about how the guy just wants to go touch Indians or something but was too emotional to tell us himself. Any questions?

3:48 P.M.: We assume he was really fired or forced to resign, so the obvious question would be, What really happened? But no one in corporate America is foolish enough to ask it. Meeting adjourned.

4:04 P.M.: After main boss leaves, employees have real meeting where they can ask all the obvious questions now that the only person who could answer them is long gone. "What the hell really happened?" someone says. "Even if I was going to go find myself I think I'd still give two weeks' notice. I mean, if you haven't found yourself by this time, what's a few more days?"

4:04:32 P.M.: Frank e-mail is in: "Remember when the days were long and rolled beneath a deep blue sky, baby? Didn't have a care in the world with Mommy and Daddy standing by, baby. But happily ever after fails, and we've been poisoned by these cuckoo-crazy fairy tales, baby. The lawyer's swell on small details, since Daddy had to fly. But I know a place where we can go that's still untouched by cats, baby." Amen, baby.

4:12 P.M.: Wife calls. Says our iguana is very ill and she wants to put it out of its misery by sticking it in a plastic bag and holding it up to the exhaust pipe of the car. Oh, that's just what I want to see when I come home—the woman I married stuffing an iguana's head in the tailpipe of our car. That's perfect, I say, realizing that I'm implementing the curve and that in this case perfect means: I married a sicko.

4:16 P.M.: Coworker who missed the big meeting comes into office. "The boss left to go touch Indians," everyone tells her. "That's interesting," she says, meaning "let's leave early."

4:21 P.M.: Before leaving I pull out that "Things To Do Before I Die" list again and make one more addition: Go touch Indians, baby.

It's a Long Way to Azerbaijan

"Don't queer my play."

—ANDY SIPOWICZ

9:21 A.M.: Two people on side of interstate are jousting with the Club. They each have one, and the duel almost looks choreographed. I pull over on the shoulder, take an apple out of my lunch box, and watch for a few minutes. It's kind of like medieval rush hour.

9:24 A.M.: Receptionist introduces me to our new temp-boss. I didn't think you could have a boss who's a temp, I say. "Oh yeah," he says.

9:44 A.M.: One of the six elevators outside our office is out of operation and won't go up or down, but the doors still open and close so some of the employees have taken to using it as sort of a decompression chamber. "I thought I was going to have a heart attack, but after four minutes in there by myself I felt like skipping rope," one worker says. "I tried to get in yesterday, but the line was too long."

9:45 A.M.: One of our new associates is standing outside the elevator right now. "I'm next. This is my third time today," she says. Don't do it too much, I tell her. At some point, you'll stop decompressing and start decomposing.

10:21 A.M.: Get long e-mail from a former associate who suddenly picked up and moved to Armenia. "It's the weekend after last week," it begins. "Am watching my satellite link with the world and it's showing some ancient American sitcom. *Evening Shade,* I think. Whatever it is, I'll be damned if Tony Bennett didn't just swing onto the screen in a bit part. He just slapped his knee."

10:43 A.M.: Coworker comes by to tell me he's just now getting into the Cure. I could tell, I say.

11:02 A.M.: Coworker who is addicted to Ramada Inn soap wants someone to drive her over to the one by the airport at lunchtime. "Why don't you just find out what kind of soap it is and buy it your- self?" someone asks. "I tried but they wouldn't tell me," she says. "Please give me a ride. I just need to tell the desk clerk there's no soap in my room, and they always give me a handful. It'll just take a minute. Please."

11:04 A.M.: Everybody feels for her, but nobody wants to go by the airport at lunchtime. "Don't they have something by the beach? I wouldn't mind taking a ride by there," one worker says.

11:17 A.M.: Read a little more about what it's like in Armenia. "Ever live in a place where degrees are counted in Celsius? It's eight here now and I'm warm as toast. Never been warm in single digits before."

11:28 A.M.: Mother calls to tell me that something is wrong with her cable. "Every channel is the Weather Channel," she says. Every channel? I say. "Every channel," she says. Can you see if it's still eight in Armenia? I ask.

11:41 A.M.: New guy passes my desk. Hey, don't queer my play, I say. "What does that mean? What'd I do?" he says. I don't know, I heard someone say it on TV and I've been desper- ate to use it ever since, I say. "You do look desperate," he says.

11:43 A.M.: Get back to perusing the customs of my Armenian friend. "I have cognac with my morning tea; am often drunk by eleven and sober by three."

11:44 A.M.: I wonder if he'd be drunk or sober now. Anybody know what time it is in Armenia? I shout out.

11:58 A.M.: Nobody knows.

12:03 P.M.: Get to decompression chamber same time as marketing guy. "We could share it," he says. No, I can't decompress with someone else, I say. "Come on, it'll be . . ." Hey, don't queer my play.

12:04 P.M.: I think it worked in that instance.

12:05 P.M.: Skip decompression and go back to reading Armenian e-mail. About halfway through it says: "Is it okay if I don't ask about how you're doing?"

12:05:17 P.M.: I think that would be wise.

12:10 P.M.: Temp-boss comes by to check on me. You know, in Armenia it's customary not to ask people how they're doing, I say. "Well, we're not in Armenia, are we?" he says. No, I say, looking up at the clock. But if we were, we'd be drunk.

12:11 P.M.: Go to lunch and eat alone.

1:04 P.M.: On way back I swing by decompression chamber. There are a few employees loitering outside it. "You don't want to go in there now," one says. "People haven't been cleaning up after themselves." I look in and see empty Pepsi One soda cans in one corner, a crumpled up Chic-Fil-A bag, and a lot of pistachio shells. "Maintenance is on their way up to clean it out. We'll let you know when she's ready," they say.

2:10 P.M.: Boss is looking for two missing employees. "They went by the beach to get some Ramada Inn soap," new guy informs him.

2:31 P.M.: Mother calls to tell me they're getting "loads of snow" in Lake Tahoe. "Lots of powder," she says.

3:01 P.M.: Browsing the Armenian e-mail, I get to the main reason he's contacted me: "You know how you can trade a pair of denim blue jeans for a car in Russia? Well, here it's spandex."

3:01:22 P.M.: "PLEASE SEND SPANDEX."

3:15 P.M.: Check on decompression chamber. It's free but reeks of hotel soap. Open doors to let it air out and head back to office.

3:27 P.M.: Message from mother on voice mail. She's so lost without her soap operas that it sounds like she's trying to conjure up situations on the Weather Channel. "I think the woman who always wears orange is sleeping with the double-breasted-suit guy," she says. "They were acting real odd, as if they were hiding something, when they were in front of the map together, especially by the Dakotas."

3:48 P.M.: Get down to end of Armenian e-mail: "Have lost fifteen pounds, down from waist size 32 to 30. I think I stepped on a land mine yesterday but nothing happened. Must be 'cause I'm so light. I live in a fourth-floor flat in a building called a 'Krushevsky' where I get water twice a day for about two hours at a time but it's usually when I'm drunk so I miss spots when I shower. Am traveling to the Iran border next week and after that to Azerbaijan."

3:49 P.M.: Head for decompression chamber. "Job getting to you?" coworker says as I pass. No, Armenia's getting to me, I say.

3:53 P.M.: No wait, so I hop right in. Just starting to decompress, I can even feel my tongue unraveling and making a squeaking noise like a New Year's Eve tooter, but then there's a jolt and the elevator is dropping rapidly.

3:54 P.M.: Tense up tongue and reel it back in just before doors open on tenth floor to pick up more passengers.

3:55 P.M.: When we reach bottom, I decide I might as well try and decompress at home.

5:12 P.M.: Head out. As I get in car, I think about how mundane things have gotten here in my America. On way home, have to stop at Kinko's and then go by the auto parts store for a new gas cap and . . .

5:13 P.M.: And after that . . . to Azerbaijan.

DAY 19

No Ice

"It's a strange invitation."

—BECK

7:50 A.M.: "Don't forget the ticket today," my wife says.

7:51 A.M.: It's a matter of hours now. This evening I'm supposed to attend the talent show at my mother-in-law's retirement complex (she's in the Daisy Duke chorus line), but due to my neglect tickets have sold out on us. Why didn't your mother get me one when she bought you one? I ask my wife for the twelfth time. "Because she thought you wouldn't want to go." She was right. "No, she wasn't."

8:19 A.M.: Guard at gate of retirement complex wants me to state my name and purpose. Tickets for the talent show, sir. "Good luck," he says, shaking his head and raising the gate.

8:23 A.M.: It can't really be sold out, I tell myself as I swing up to the clubhouse. Inside the door a guy is sitting in a metal folding chair with a piece of rope, making knots. "Making knots," he says, looking up.

8:24 A.M.: I explain my situation. "How many do you need?" he says. Just one, I say. "That's not going to be easy," he says.

8:29 A.M.: After about the third knot he tells me he can't really help me at all. "Well, actually anybody could help you, but Gladys has to," he says.

8:30 A.M.: "But she's long gone." Passed away? I question delicately.

8:30:12 A.M.: "Day trip," he says.

8:30:34 A.M.: But it's only 8:30, are you sure they've left? "Left at dawn," he says. Dawn? How far did they have to go?

8:31 A.M.: "Four miles."

8:42 A.M.: Seems the town's public works department is having an open house where they bring in all the heavy equipment and trucks and let the retirees sit in them and stuff. I pull in and park next to one of those meter maid three-wheelers. There must be nine people in it. It's loaded like one of those circus cars full of little people only it's full of old people.

8:49 A.M.: Ask if anyone has seen Gladys. "I think she's by the dump trucks," someone tells me. "She's wearing a striped top with solid slacks."

9:02 A.M.: Gladys? "No." Gladys? "No." Gladys? "No."

9:31 A.M.: Giving rides in cherry picker. Go up with a guy named Merril. "Your shoes look comfortable," he says. Look out over the crowd. Lots of striped tops. Lots of solid slacks. Gladys? "No."

9:51 A.M.: On ride to work I remember talking to a lady in clubhouse yesterday to see if I could order one ticket over the phone. "Much easier if you just stop by," she said.

10:34 A.M.: It's Tenant Appreciation Day at work. Landlord is going all out. Lots of activity in lobby of building. Clowns and such.

10:46 A.M.: Get face painted.

11:18 A.M.: Message on voice mail. "Did you get a ticket?" wife says.

12:03 P.M.: Call back and tell her I'll just get one at

the door. No problem. "I bet," she says. "And don't forget we have to go by that party my friend from work is having afterward. I told Mary we'd at least stop by." Couldn't we just drive by?

12:44 P.M.: Word is landlord has put out a huge spread of food in the lobby now. But when I get there all it is . . . is hot dogs. Thousands of them. Standing up. A sign flashes in my head: When you really want to show your appreciation, show it with hot dogs.

12:47 P.M.: Pass on the franks, but take a roll as a souvenir. Go to lunch and eat alone.

1:16 P.M.: Stop eating alone. Guy who is very upset sits down next to me on a bench beside the New River. "My boss is a belligerent jerk," he says. "He treats me like I'm stupid. I'm not an idiot. I have an IQ."

1:17 P.M.: I nod. "I can read," he says. And that's when it starts. "Ladybug," he says as the first boat passes. "Silver Shalis," he says as the next one glides by. He can read.

1:18 P.M.: "Nice 'n' Easy," he says. "Isn't that the name of the hair coloring stuff?" Yes, I think you're right, I say. "They stole it," he says.

1:20 P.M.: "Sea Snatch," he says. I have to go get a hot dog for this bun, I say.

1:58 P.M.: Get back to work. Wife calls. "You haven't left yet?" Left? The show's not until tonight. "You know their night's different than ours. Doors open at 4:05." I'll meet you there, I say. "You better be there."

3:40 P.M.: Traffic heading out west to the condo complex is all blocked up, as if I'm heading toward a giant arena or something. Everybody has their lights on.

3:46 P.M.: What if I really can't get a ticket and I have to stand out front waiting for a condo scalper, standing there with one finger raised high above the stooping crowd, hoping for a miracle.

4:12 P.M.: There are no seats but Gladys agrees to let me stand off by the refreshment table, which works out well, since my mother-in-law wants me to get her a Coke "with no ice." I thought you wouldn't have to say that in a retirement community, I tell her. I thought it would just be automatic. In fact, I thought it worked the opposite. That if you wanted ice you'd have to make a special request, maybe even a written request in triplicate with two days' notice.

4:43 P.M.: "Just get it," she says. "And get me some of those chocolate chip cookies with no chips in them and one of those ice cream pops without the stick, just put it in a bowl. No stick," she yells after me.

4:52 P.M.: "Where's my change?" she says as I return. No change, I say.

6:10 P.M.: The show moves rather quickly. The mother-in-law does a few high kicks and then lowers into sort of an Elvis Presley "Suspicious Minds" karate crouch before collapsing onstage.

7:02 P.M.: Slip out when Gladys puts on blackface and starts singing "Mammy, oh, mammy."

7:54 P.M.: Party Number Two is very crowded. Woman we know is rushing up to the house. "I would have been here sooner but I made Mary a birthday card with my Print Shop on the computer," she says. "That's cute," my wife says. That's crap, I say. It was cute in '89. Don't look at me like that, I say to my wife. She needs to know if it's going to be her excuse for being late to parties and whatnot. Look at it. It's all faded and the candles look like pink fire hydrants.

8:01 P.M.: Go directly for bookcase at party. It's improper social etiquette to go to someone's house and just sit in a corner and read a magazine, but if you go and start looking through their books people assume you're just investigating your host's taste in literature.

8:46 P.M.: Mary's taste in literature is crap, I tell my wife.

9:41 P.M.: Uh-oh, the guy who always tries to get me to change my personal convictions about . . . everything is heading over with his girlfriend, who has this annoying habit of taking sole possession of everyday things and claiming them for her own . . . "Oh, I have to have my Dunkin' Donuts Coffee Colada or I'm a monster in the morning; Oh, if it wasn't for my Y-100 radio station and that Zoo Crew I don't think I could stand the drive to work; Oh, I can't live without my Target."

9:42 P.M.: "Oh, if my *Frasier* wasn't a rerun tonight I wouldn't be here," she says. Oh, if I could just be back up in my cherry picker right now, looking for Gladys and discussing comfortable shoes with Merril.

9:45 P.M.: "So . . ." the conviction buster says, "what have you been doing lately?" Just ignoring my armpits, I say. "No, really?" he says. And I just decide to give it all up on the spot. It's no use with this guy. I have like two reasons for all my convictions put together. He has like forty-five against each of them. Okay, I say. Abortion is bad, the death penalty is good, and Garth Brooks is all right.

9:48 P.M.: Whew, I never knew I had so much to give up. But even this isn't good enough for him.

9:48:14 P.M.: "Why?" he says.

9:48:15 P.M.: "Ooooh," his girlfriend says tugging him into the next room. Somebody made artichoke dip. "You know how I love my artichoke dip." "You're still a Cat Stevens fan, aren't you?" he yells to me as she hauls him away.

10:02 P.M.: Two teenage girls are in a back room watching TV. The screen is blood red. What's that you're watching? I ask. "Satan Channel," they say. I assume they're putting me on, but then a commercial comes on. It's for hot dogs.

10:04 P.M.: Go by the coolers, where a guy is fishing out beers. "Molson or Molson Ice?" he says. No ice, I say.

10:07 P.M.: Duck out on patio. I had so much moral conviction an hour ago and now I have nothing. Feels good.

10:09 P.M.: On the steps going into the yard there's a couple of potted plants and some frayed twine they used to hang from. I sit down and a little girl in a blue velvety dress comes up behind me. "What's that on your face?" she says. It's a moon and stars, I tell her. "What are you doing now?" she asks.

10:10 P.M.: I'm making knots.

DAY 20

Appraising the Damage

"Oh, what a sweet evening this is."

—LEWIS

7:58 A.M.: Can't believe I have to get up and work on a Saturday.

7:59 A.M.: Believe it.

8:04 A.M.: Go to mailbox to get yesterday's mail. Open up a brochure for night classes at the community school and there on page three, amidst Guitar 1 and Calligraphy 17, is Auto Damage Appraisal. I've been waiting for something like this because every time I have to fill out one of those forms that says, "Tell us one thing that nobody knows about you," I can't come up with the one thing. But now I can see myself boldly writing in: "Can appraise auto damage."

8:05 A.M.: Neighbor who only watches PBS and is always full of historical facts rushes over to the border of my property, stops short, and yells, "Did you know Lewis and Clark were gay?" That explains everything, I say.

8:12 A.M.: As I'm pulling out of my block another neighbor who just took up jogging stops me at the corner by stepping in front of my car and motioning for me to roll down my window. "My wife says these shorts make me look like I have Richard Simmons legs. Tell me I don't have Richard Simmons legs," he says. I can't do that, I say.

9:38 A.M.: At work temp-boss comes over with old boss's planner and says he has to check with me about something called timelines. "Are they still not about anything important?" he asks. Well, I say, they were supposed to be whimsical and enlightening but now they're just about ex-cons and armpits. "Okay," he says. "I'll check back in a week."

10:50 A.M.: Call my brother to remind him that my parents need to be picked up at the airport this evening. "Tell me something I don't know," he groans. Lewis and Clark were gay, I say.

11:02 A.M.: Coworker is complaining that someone called him and said, "Hey, I guess we were playing phone tag." But he wasn't. "I think people just like to say it but I wasn't playing with him," he says adamantly.

11:05 A.M.: Phone tag has become tiring to him but I admit that I've never played and that makes me sad. We decide the best way for me to get into the game would be to call people at lunchtime. "Nobody will be there," he says.

12:15 P.M.: Make five phone calls and leave messages with two answering machines and three secretaries and then run out of the office in case anyone tries to call back right away.

12:21 P.M.: Go to lunch, expecting to eat alone.

12:34 P.M.: The inside of McDonald's is extremely crowded. All the registers are going and you can't quite tell where the lines begin and end. It looks like a fast-food mosh pit.

12:40 P.M.: Customers are getting bored and making small talk with all the wrong people. "The stock market is going crazy. How you making out?" a guy reading a newspaper asks me. I'm wearing my investments, I say. The shoes are long term.

12:42 P.M.: A lot of workers are moving around behind the counter but nobody seems to be getting their orders filled.

12:46 P.M.: An older couple is getting grumpy. "This is ridiculous, I'm gonna say something," the husband says to his wife. "Why do you always have to be the one to say something?" the wife says. "Let somebody else be the one."

12:47 P.M.: "I'll be the one," a woman who is squashed up against them says. "Hey, what the heck's going on here?" she shouts.

12:47:03 P.M.: And then everybody is the one. It's a room full of ones. "Yeah." "Yeah!" "Yeah." "Yeah, what's going on?"

12:48 P.M.: "They're giving the drive-through customers preferential treatment," says a kid in line. "It's bad for business to have fifty cars jammed up in your parking lot honking their horns and blocking traffic, so they take care of them first. When it gets busy, the clerks are told to let the inside people suffer."

12:49 P.M.: "How do you know that?" a woman asks the boy. "It's in the training films of every fast-food place I've ever worked at," he says. "Except for Arby's, 'cause they never have lines anyway, nobody ever goes there. Oh, and they always put the smartest people in the drive-through, too. The person with the headset is always the genius of the crew."

12:49:07 P.M.: "Did you wear a headset?" I ask him. "Only when a lot of people called in sick," he says.

12:49:12 P.M.: "Is this true? They have training films telling you to take care of the outside people first?" a woman in the back says to a clerk. "We see a lotta films, ma'am," the clerk says, picking up two cheeseburgers and handing them to a head-setted woman.

12:50 P.M.: Head out to the car and zip through drive-through.

1:27 P.M.: Two male smokers are standing outside our office building questioning their manhood because they can't stop watching *Ally McBeal* and *Sex in the City.* They decide it's okay. "Funny is funny," one guy says. "But if you catch me trying to buy tickets to a Sarah McLachlan concert, shoot me."

2:02 P.M.: Coworker who's in trouble with his spouse corners me to ask if I keep any secrets from my wife. Only the fact that I can appraise auto damage, I say.

2:30 P.M.: Phone is ringing like crazy but I just let voice mail pick it up. I'm being tagged like crazy. I'm it!

3:12 P.M.: Guy in men's room is holding his stomach. "Concentrate," he says. "I drank cranberry concentrate. It looked like a regular bottle of juice but it makes sixty-four ounces. It was a little thick when I first tasted it but you know juices." I know juices, I say.

3:13 P.M.: "Ahh," he says bending over in pain. "I can't believe I did this to myself. I feel so thick. I can't think of anything worse."

3:13:19 P.M.: You could have Richard Simmons legs, I say.

4:10 P.M.: Game time. Make first call back. "We must be playing phone tag," the voice on the other end says. The bastard beat me to it. I wanted to be the one to say it. I don't want to play with you, I say, hanging up.

5:12 P.M.: Feel a bit displaced, as if I no longer belong where I am in life. Not that there's a major change in order but just that I should be like maybe a few feet over to the left or at least closer to the exit.

5:13 P.M.: Exit.

6:01 P.M.: Pickup truck in front of me on highway has a SAFETY FIRST—BUCKLE UP bumper sticker on the tailgate. In the back of the truck are about eight kids in Little League uniforms standing up and falling into each other as the truck cruises along at fifty miles an hour.

8:40 P.M.: Have the second part of Lewis and Clark documentary on tape that neighbor loaned me. Pop it in and wait for something to happen.

9:40 P.M.: Narrator says: "January 20, nothing material occurred worth mentioning."

10:10 P.M.: After the expedition is over things start picking up. Lewis is all wasted on methadone and opium and looking for a good place to kill himself, and Clark is having an argument with York, the personal slave who blazed across the country with him. Now that they've all returned to praise and fanfare, and all the members of the discovery crew are being rewarded with cushy government jobs and big plots of land, York wants to know why he's still Clark's slave. Clark is furious and writes a letter to a friend saying, "York is getting uppity."

10:11 P.M.: I wonder if Clark would have acted differently if York was gay.

10:40 P.M.: Set my alarm for the middle of the night so I can call a couple of people and leave messages on their machines and get a head start on playing tag tomorrow.

Nada

Nothing material occurred worth mentioning.

Ode to a Jamoch

*"I see, and sing, by my own eyes inspired. So let
me be the choir and make a moan."*

—FROM "ODE TO PSYCHE" BY JOHN KEATS

8:31 A.M.: Trying to write an ode but can't think of who or what I feel that strongly about. Tried a generic ode to a lass but got nowhere. There is only one person I seem to be able to muster up enough passion and praise for, but the title just doesn't sing when I put pen to paper.

8:32 A.M.: "Ode to Christopher Walken."

8:45 A.M.: Every sink in the house is talking back: burping, spraying, gushing. I had seen our ex-con house guest messing around with one of the spouts a couple of days earlier, but I thought it was just some kind of perverted thing so I didn't question him for fear of hearing the answer. But now that the front of my pants are all wet I have to get to the bottom of this.

8:46 A.M.: He's sleeping. Jumps up when he sees me standing in the middle of his room yelling, My pants are all wet!

8:46:04 A.M.: Ask him if he knows what's going on with the water faucets. "Oh, I didn't think it would matter," he says. What? What wouldn't matter? "I needed the little screens for my pipe."

8:47 A.M.: *For my pipe.* Those three words just linger in the air for a few moments and then it dawns on me . . . He's taken the little screens out of the spigots to use in his pot pipe. Stripping a man's faucets for his personal paraphernalia. Hey, what the hell do you think you're doing? I say.

8:49 A.M.: He's asleep again.

8:49:07 A.M.: I start to jostle him. I want my screens back. Where are they? "I don't think they'll fit," he says, rolling over. "I kind of customized them." You customized my spigot screens?

8:50 A.M.: You sick bastard. Now I've got to go to the hardware store. I was going to write an ode this morning. "A what?" he says. An ode! I say, getting in his face.

9:07 A.M.: On way to hardware store I think about how cool it would be to give someone an uppercut to the jaw right after you scream, "An ode!" What a missed opportunity.

9:12 A.M.: In front of hardware store two guys are standing by their car with jumbo coffees resting on the roof and laughing their heads off. "What a jamoch," one guy howls.

9:13 A.M.: I've been hearing people use that expression for years and they look like the type of guys who would actually be able to tell me what a jamoch is (and maybe even how to spell it) but I let them get away. Another missed opportunity.

9:15 A.M.: Goofy guy at counter tells me they don't have any little screens. "Just big ones," he says. But I'm afraid he might have been the jamoch the other guys were referring to so I check for myself.

9:38 A.M.: On ride to work I dwell on how the car's console has so many fake buttons where real buttons would be if I had all the options. I never minded when there was just like a cutout where the clock was supposed to be because who needs a clock but these facsimiles kind of taunt you. "I could be a sunroof," one says to me slyly and I press on it until my thumb hurts.

9:41 A.M.: Think about writing "Ode to the Options I Could Have Had If I'd Leased."

10:18 A.M.: "There's someone I want you to meet," the boss says. "Come on, and try to make a good first impression." I don't like to make first impressions, I say. In fact, I'm working on a way to make only second impressions, but I haven't perfected it yet.

10:19 A.M.: Nice to meet you, I say. "Same here," she says, extending her hand and looking down at my wet pants. Houseguest stripped my spigot screens to use in his pot pipes and it's a long story, I say. "Jesus," my boss says, shaking his head.

10:40 A.M.: I'm sure it's an Italian thing. Look up Italian names in phone book and call one at random to ask if they know what a jamoch is. Person who picks up says, "Thanks, but we don't need any right now," and hangs up.

10:42 A.M.: Call a Garb Piazzano. "I'm not Italian," he says.

10:43 A.M.: "You're a head case," coworker says to me.

10:44 A.M.: "Ode to a Head Case." I like that.

11:22 A.M.: Guy in office wants to know why he can't get in as good shape as the gay guys he knows. I don't think there's like any sort of special secret gay exercise regimen, if that's what you mean, I say. "I go to the same gym with gay guys," he says. "I'm doing the same exercises, drinking the same Orange Julius. But at the end of the day they look so damn taut and tight I can't even compare. It's not fair."

11:24 A.M.: Maybe they're just born that way, I say.

12:18 P.M.: Go to lunch to eat alone.

12:32 P.M.: There's some kind of jam up in drive-through line and I get a bit claustrophobic. After several minutes of clutching and inching and idling and staring down the button that keeps saying, "I could be an ejector seat," I get out of the car. "What are you doing?" woman in car behind me asks. I'm stretching my legs. "Oh," she says, climbing out of her car. Turn around so the front of my pants, which are still a little damp, can face the sun.

12:41 P.M.: Guy in Lincoln Navigator suddenly lurches and climbs the curb, breaking free of the drive-through line. "And they said I'd never use my four-wheel drive in Florida," he says out the window.

12:53 P.M.: The atmosphere is starting to remind me of one of those scenes in a movie when a freeway is suddenly shut down and people get out and start milling around. Guy three cars back stands on hood of his car to see if he can see what's going on at the front of the line. He yells something about a deep fryer but I can't hear him over the hum of the helicopters circling above us.

12:59 P.M.: Get back in car to rest my legs.

1:21 P.M.: Catch a well-known Italian guy smoking in front of our building. He's more than happy to tell me what a jamoch is. "You know," he says, "it's like a galoot, a clumsy galoot." But what's a galoot, exactly? "You know, a big galoot," he says. But then what's a little galoot? "I don't know," he says.

1:24 P.M.: What a jamoch, I mutter to myself as I walk away.

1:38 P.M.: Coworker tells me I should call her doctor about my health problems. "He won't even make you come in. He'll just give you something," she says. What do you mean give me something? "You know . . . something?"

1:40 P.M.: Oh no, I don't need anything to lift my mental state, I say. What is this world coming to? I just need someone to talk to.

1:49 P.M.: Call coworker's doctor.

2:10 P.M.: Wife calls to tell me we need some new shower curtain rings. Half are missing. How do they get off the bar? I ask. "I don't know, it's like magic," she says.

2:34 P.M.: Guy who wants to be as fit as his gay friends wants to shave his armpit hair. That's not the answer, I tell him. "It has nothing to do with that," he says. "I just want your blessing. Everybody's doing it. Pit hair is in for girls. Out for guys." Okay, you have my blessing.

3:10 P.M.: Decide to spend the rest of the afternoon working on an ode that wallows in missed opportunities, second impressions, and hairless blessings.

3:10:41 P.M.: Working title: "Ode to a Little Galoot."

5:28 P.M.: Stop at place called Uncle Sam's on way home. I've never been in a head shop before. Lots of Grateful Dead posters and gargoyle candles. Yeah, that's what I'm looking for, I tell the clerk, "How many?" he says. Mmm (kitchen, two bathrooms . . .), a bag of four is good, I say. "Okay, anything else?" he asks.

5:30 P.M.: Yes, actually, if you've got any drug paraphernalia that could double as a shower curtain ring, it would save me another stop.

5:31 P.M.: Oh, and do you have those springy things that go behind doors so they don't hit the wall?

DAY 23

The Dark Hand of Chance

"Stay with me."

—PAT RILEY

9:44 A.M.: As soon as I get to work one of our interns comes over with a grocery store receipt from Tamarac that reads: ZORRO WAS YOUR CASHIER TODAY.

9:44:36 A.M.: Are you going to give me that or are you just showing it to me? "I'm just showing," she says. Well, will you help me get one? "Yes, yes I will," she says.

9:44:54 A.M.: Okay, I'm going to need a map because navigating the retirement community at Tamarac can get . . . what's the word I'm looking for?

9:45 A.M.: "Tricky," she says.

9:46 A.M.: Yes, Tamarac can get tricky. And do you know what hours Zorro works? "No." Do you know if he's one of those stockmen that only mans the register when it's busy because I've run into that before and it can make things very difficult. "I don't know," she says. Well, find out.

10:12 A.M.: Finally, someone in the sports world has decided to bring the sport quote out of the realm of repetitive nonsense. See in the paper that when asked about a recent win Pat Riley doesn't say, "It was a great team effort" or "We made some big plays." No, he says: "Maybe it was preordained today in the universe. There's three things at work, there's the dark hand of chance—stay with me—and then there's luck in one circle and then there's force."

10:14 A.M.: I wonder what it would be like if our employees had to be interviewed after work every day and asked about how well or badly they excelled. Would the replies be insightful and mystical like Riley's or would they too just sound like simpletons?

10:41 A.M.: Boss comes out to let us know there's a big meeting scheduled for this afternoon at 3:15. Oh, a big event. Follow boss back and ask him if I can interview everyone after big meeting. "At this point, anything you do is a plus," he says, waving me off.

11:01 A.M.: Get another e-mail from former associate who is now living in Armenia. All it says is: "I finally met a girl but her name scares me."

11:02 A.M.: How could a name really turn you off? In grade school I myself once held hands with a girl named Phyllis at the same time Cloris Leachman had a sitcom of the same name and it hardly bothered me, except on Tuesdays.

11:03 A.M.: E-mail him back asking for more details and, by the way, what time is it in Armenia?

11:11 A.M.: Word is they've got some kind of new futuristic vending machine in the break room. "You press a button and stuff like hot soft pretzels, double-cheese grilled cheese sandwiches, fish sticks, and omelets on a bun just pop out all cooked," someone says. "At least that's what I hear."

11:14 A.M.: Me and new guy head down to see if what people are hearing is true. When we arrive the door to the new machine is flung wide open and a vendor mechanic is reading the owner's manual.

11:14:39 A.M.: "We hear this machine is amazing," new guy says. Vendor mechanic looks up and then proudly shows us how the packaged item drops into this small compartment and is ripped open by tiny robotic hands. "And then it gets sucked into an internal microwave—stay with me—that's deep inside. I've never even seen it," he says. "Then it travels through this tunnel and pops out here steaming hot." Very futuristic, I say. "It's not working," he says.

11:16 A.M.: "Very today," the new guy says.

11:16:12 A.M.: What's wrong? we ask. "Someone got a pretzel-and-egg sandwich," he says, turning to the troubleshooting section of his manual. On page seven in boldface type it says: "If Someone Gets a Pretzel-and-Egg Sandwich."

11:17 A.M.: He thinks the glitch has something to do with the new eggs being odorless. Is that good? I ask. I know I once read that the better the rose the less the smell but I don't think that goes for eggs too. "It's good," he says. "Someday nothing will smell."

11:17:07 A.M.: Wow, we say.

11:18 A.M.: Well, we'll come back when she's up and running, I say. "Give me a couple of hours," the vendor says, getting down on all fours.

11:21 A.M.: "What was it like?" someone asks when we get back to the office. We've seen the future, I say, and it smells like odorless eggs.

11:21:22 A.M.: "Someday," the new guy says, "nothing will smell."

12:17 P.M.: Go to lunch and eat alone.

1:06 P.M.: Guy with a beard and ponytail is sitting by the river with a guitar playing "Stairway to Heaven." Ask him to stop but he won't.

1:21 P.M.: When I get back from lunch there is a street map of Tamarac on my desk. I don't know why anyone would use an intern for sex when you can get them to do stuff like this.

2:39 P.M.: Armenian e-mail arrives: "I have no idea what time it is in Armenia. As far as the woman goes—she's sassy, delightful, tall, and frightening when I have to call her name out in the dark."

2:41 P.M.: E-mail him back: Cut the crap. What's her name?

2:48 P.M.: Good news. Exceptional news. Ex-con house-guest calls to tell me he went to court today and has to begin serving a sentence in a couple of days and he wants to know if I can give him a ride tonight to pick up some "essentials" he's going to need in the lock-up. Whoa! I say what's this all about?

2:49 P.M.: The intro to his story is barely intelligible but it appears that a few weeks before he moved in with us he had been approached in a bar and asked if he wanted to buy some pot. So what'd you do? I ask. "I said no but I . . ." You what?

2:51 P.M.: "I sniffed," he says. "Like this . . ."

2:51:06 P.M.: Sniffs.

2:51:32 P.M.: Seems that's the signal for cocaine. "Yeah, but get this," he says, getting all indignant. "They bring me crack. I don't want crack. I say, 'What's this?' and throw it on the ground. But the undercover cops arrest me anyway. That's not right, man." Let me get this straight, I say. You think you shouldn't have been arrested because you ordered cocaine and they brought you crack?

2:53 P.M.: "Hey, I ain't no crackhead," he says.

2:53:12 P.M.: And I ain't no taxi service, I say, hanging up.

2:54 P.M.: "Who was that?" the new guy asks me. Some crackhead, I say.

3:15 P.M.: Big meeting is supposed to start.

3:27 P.M.: Meeting really starts.

4:17 P.M.: Meeting ends.

4:19 P.M.: We don't have a locker room, so I follow some coworkers into restroom. "What are you doing?" one of the supervisors says. I just have a few questions. You seemed kind of timid in the meeting today, not quite as opinionated as usual. Did you go into the meeting feeling that you had nothing to prove? "Get the hell out of here," she says.

4:22 P.M.: Head over to men's restroom and catch marketing guy on his way out. "I think we just did what we had to do," marketing guy says. You've never done that before, I say. I have to ask you, why today? "I have no comment to that," he says. Okay, how 'bout this, I say . . .

4:23 P.M.: Why tomorrow?

4:24 P.M.: Inside everyone is talking about the art guy. "He was awesome," the guys by the sinks tell me. "He exceeded standards. That's the first time we've ever seen anyone do that."

4:24:06 P.M.: Catch up to art guy and go to shake his hand. "Let me just wash my hands first," he says. So, I say, the presentation you made was riveting. How'd you feel about it? "You know a lot of people would have given up, would have quit. But we ain't going out like that."

4:25 P.M.: Tell art guy that I heard the woman who was supposed to make the presentation with him today was out sick and may be out for the next two or three days. Is there anything you'd want to say to her?

4:25:09 P.M.: "This one's for you, Phyllis."

4:26 P.M.: "Will you let me get my pants up first," new guy says. That's okay, I say, in the pros the guys are usually naked when they comment. You were very "only meets standards" out there today, I tell him. "I just wasn't on today. It happens," he says. That's awfully cavalier of you, I say. "I'll pick up around salary time," he says.

4:27 P.M.: "It was a great effort all around," the other marketing guy tells me. Yeah, yeah, I say. But was there anything preordained today in the universe? The dark hand of chance, perhaps? "Get out of my way," he says, pushing past me.

4:27:34 P.M.: I used to think it was just that pro athletes were vapid and repetitive, but it's about the same here.

4:28 P.M.: Hey, here comes the big guy. Ask boss if he's got a minute to comment. "Sure, you mind if I take a dump while we talk?" No, no, that's cool.

4:32 P.M.: When I get back to my desk there's a Post-it that reads: "Zorro off Tues. and Thurs."

4:38 P.M.: Head out with new guy to see if the future is still broken.

4:44 P.M.: Machine looks like it's ready to go but looking at the menu we're not so sure. Splitting fries sounds cool. "Hey, let's split some fries." But who wants to be the guinea pig for vending-machine fries? We opt for the pretzel. "What's the worst that can happen?" new guys says. We get a pretzel-and-egg sandwich? I say.

4:46 P.M.: A light flashes saying the food is being prepped and it sounds more like Benihana in there than the future, lots of chopping sounds, *chop, chop, chop* . . .

4:47:16 P.M.: Pop. "Not exactly Jetson food," the new guy says, holding it up to the light.

4:48:49 P.M.: I don't see any salt on it, do you? "You think those bumps are salt?" Maybe the salt is on the inside, that would make it super-futuristic. "Yeah, but there's only one way to find out." You mean take a bite out of that?

4:49 P.M.: We both take one more hard look at it.

4:51 P.M.: "Wanna split some fries?" new guy says.

4:52 P.M.: Put money in for fries but while it's prepping we have second thoughts and flee, running from the future.

5:06 P.M.: Back in office get final e-mail from Armenia and it leaves me breathless.

5:06:02 P.M.: "Kevorkian."

Day 24

The Back Way

"He's not a prisoner; he's a patient."

—Barry Levine

8:21 A.M.: Read article about how doctors have decided that, after years of therapy, Reagan's would-be assassin John Hinckley is now ready to have dinner with friends at a private home. What is wrong in this world that someone like Hinckley has friends and I don't?

8:41 A.M.: Phone rings. It's our ex-con houseguest who stayed with friends last night. This is the week he's supposed to report to jail for thirty days for buying crack from undercover cops when he actually wanted to buy cocaine. "They tricked me," he said at the time. But this call isn't about that. "I got jumped," he says.

8:41:17 A.M.: Honey, he got jumped—ten guys, I shout to my wife. "What was he doing?" she says. What were you doing? I ask him. "I was just standing there doing nothing," he says. He was just standing there doing nothing, I tell my wife. "That figures," she says.

8:42 A.M.: "How was he wearing his baseball cap?" she asks. "Was it backward or was it sideways?"

8:42:14 A.M.: "Sideways."

8:42:23 A.M.: He got what he deserved.

8:44 A.M.: He starts going on about how his head is split open and he lost one of his front teeth. I have two words for you, I say.

8:44:17 A.M.: Butterflies and gold.

8:44:36 A.M.: "But . . ."

8:44:38 A.M.: I gotta go, I say. Call me later at work. At least then I'll be getting paid to talk to you.

9:49 A.M.: They've installed a security camera outside the entrance to our office and you now need a special card to get in but nobody has a card so we're all locked out, standing in the hallway looking up at the monitor. "Whose job is it to watch the monitor?" someone asks. "Mine," a voice behind me says.

9:52 A.M.: This is so people don't come in the office and shoot us, someone says. "Well, somebody better let us in because we're sitting ducks out here," new guy says.

9:54 A.M.: Marketing person says she knows a back way in and everyone follows her. After we get in we all have to file past the boss's office. "Where's everybody coming from?" he says. We came in the back way, I say. "That's cool," he says. "I didn't know we had a back way."

10:15 A.M.: After we get settled in I tell new guy that I have so few acquaintances that even if I accused certain people of being my friends and had them all over for a private dinner there wouldn't even be enough of them for passing. The table and setting would be so small there would be none of that, "Can you pass me the potatoes?" "Oh, could someone send me that gravy down here?" It would all just be there, within reach. No passing.

10:16 A.M.: "No passing?" he says.

10:16:44 A.M.: No passing, I say.

10:17 A.M.: "Hinckley would have passing," he says.

10:41 A.M.: Ex-con calls. Tells me he's all worried about his appearance because he has to report to prison tomorrow. What are you worried about? I say. It's not like you're going to a wedding on Saturday. You're going to prison. Who the hell cares how you look? "I don't want to go in a beaten man," he says.

10:43 A.M.: Accidentally hang up on him but it was a good line to close on anyway.

10:45 A.M.: Boss asks monitor watcher if she's had much action out in the hallway. She takes eyes off the monitor for a second and says, "Just watching the carpet grow."

10:47 A.M.: Ask boss how it's supposed to be handled if some stranger shows up at the door unannounced. "We ask them what they want?" he says. And what if they want me? "Then we'll say you're busy right now but they can make an appointment," he says. So people can't just walk in to kill me but they can make an appointment to kill me? "Basically."

10:48 A.M.: Go out back way to use the bathroom.

11:01 A.M.: Ex-con is back on the line. Are you sure it was ten guys? I ask. Because sometimes when you're on the ground and people are kicking you all those shoes make it seem like more than it actually is. Did you really have the presence of mind to count how many people were beating you? "Maybe it was seven," he says.

11:02 A.M.: What do you pack for prison? I ask. Can you bring conditioner?

11:03 A.M.: He accidentally hangs up on me. I think.

11:23 A.M.: Monitor watcher says she's tired of talking on the speaker to people out in the hall. "I feel like a fast-food worker," she says.

11:47 A.M.: Security has now sealed off our secret back way entrance so camera-shy employees have stopped going to the bathroom. "I got out but I couldn't get back in," the marketing guy is crying. The odds of getting shot in the workplace are like 44 million to one so this doesn't make sense compared to the odds of having to go to the bathroom, I explain to the boss. "We took that into account," he says. "Safety first. Bathroom second."

12:10 P.M.: Go to lunch with the very real intention that I will never return.

12:18 P.M.: Eat alone at a pizza place that has a giant map of Long Island covering an entire wall. Sit under my hometown.

12:41 P.M.: Hear a voice in my head say, "Isn't it ironic that he was shot directly under his hometown?" Move to Montauk Point. Not because I'm really afraid of being shot under my hometown but because I'm not sure if that is the correct use of *ironic*.

1:04 P.M.: Think about a book I was reading about pararescue jumpers who save people at sea. During training, the sergeant throws a whistle into the bottom of a pool and has ten guys fight over it. The first guy that comes up with it blows the whistle and then gets out of the pool. They keep doing this until only one person is left and that person gets cut from the squad and sent packing.

1:06 P.M.: I have no doubt I'd be the last guy but I wonder if I would get to keep the whistle.

1:18 P.M.: Run into former boss on walk back to office. "Terry, how's life treating you?" he says. I'm not on a par with John Hinckley as far as social interaction but I'm trying, I say. "Good," he says.

1:31 P.M.: Catch office door as someone else is coming out. Whew!

1:31:17 P.M.: "Lucky bastard," someone says. Not really, I say. I just remembered I have to go to the bathroom.

2:16 P.M.: Come across a list of this week's Top Ten songs. Number eight is "Invasion of the Flat Booty."

3:01 P.M.: Staff members who are afraid to go to the bathroom are getting jittery. One woman, who is usually very calm, is frantically pacing back and forth in front of her desk while trying to talk on the phone. After she hangs up I ask her, Isn't it murder trying to hold it? "I'm just thankful to be alive," she says.

3:54 P.M.: Wife calls to tell me she feels sorry about the ex-con having to go into prison a beaten man. "Sure he's a criminal, but he was our criminal," she says. I guess we can't call him ex-con anymore. Now it's just con, I say.

4:02 P.M.: Monitor watcher who has been made to feel like fast-food worker is wearing a hair net now.

4:28 P.M.: Problem solved. After the week-long installation of three thousand dollars in security equipment, the hiring of two monitor watchers, the sealing off of one back way, the pain involved with four blown bladders and the purchase of one hair net, someone has stuck a chair outside to hold front doors open. "Bathroom first. Safety second," someone says.

5:01 P.M.: Phone rings. It's our con telling me the real reason he's been calling is there is a weekly fee of fourteen dollars when he goes into jail. Prison rent? What's the worst that can happen if you don't pay? I ask. They evict you from prison?

5:03 P.M.: "Very funny," he says. "They can really make life miserable for me. Can I borrow some money or not?" Are you kidding? I say. That is a bargain. As long as you're not going to be living with us I'm happy to help you out. Do they have any kind of rent-to-own deals? I mean, I'd even be willing to cosign if they have some kind of thirty-year mortgage plan . . .

5:05 P.M.: And if you ever get out you have to promise to come over for a private dinner.

I Am Not, I Said

"Oh, they tell me of an uncloudy day."

—WILLIE NELSON

8:13 A.M.: Everything's changed. Everything looks so good to me today. You look like you've been airbrushed, I tell my wife. "Oh, that's nice," she says.

8:13:44 A.M.: Yeah, it is. It really is.

8:22 A.M.: My breakfast looks like a picture of a breakfast in a magazine. It appears to be shellacked and sprayed with something to keep it alive and vibrant under the hot lights.

8:23 A.M.: Get camera and take photo of breakfast.

8:24 A.M.: Snap a second shot just to be sure.

8:41 A.M.: See new neighbor getting into her car. She's wearing a very smart royal blue suit with iridescent shoes. Tell her she looks like a shiny Macintosh apple with a tiny dull spot. I want to rub you on my shirt, I yell over. "Stay where you are," she screams.

9:38 A.M.: Minivan in front of me on highway has a license plate frame that says, "I'd rather be at a Neil Diamond concert" and the personalized plate reads: IM-ISAID.

9:41 A.M.: Wonder if SHILOH is taken.

9:43 A.M.: What a day. Stop to get some more film. You know how they talk about Kodak moments, I tell the clerk, how most people have to wait for these little highlights and get like one or two in a lifetime and they're lucky if the flash is working? "Yes," she says. Well, all my moments are like that now.

9:44 A.M.: "Then how come you're buying Fuji film?" she asks. Did I say Kodak moments? I meant Fuji moments.

9:44:12 A.M.: They're more intense.

10:02 A.M.: In elevator at work the buttons are glowing like majestic embers in a king's hearth.

10:02:12 A.M.: Use shirt sleeves as sort of a pot holder and press 12.

10:04 A.M.: The pen on my desk is glistening like a maestro's baton on the upstroke.

10:07 A.M.: Boss comes by. Looks like he just took his hairpiece in for a tune-up and he seems very pleased to see me. "Hey, Terry," he says. "That's the first time I've seen you pick up a pen in weeks." Isn't it beautiful, I say.

10:08 A.M.: Make note in my journal: *Medication must be working.*

10:12 A.M.: Even my armpits look skinny today.

10:14 A.M.: Or maybe it's not so much the medication as the joyous thought of knowing that our ex-con is going back in the clinker.

10:17 A.M.: Former coworker who's been in rehab for the past three weeks calls. I thought you weren't going to call anymore because you could only use the pay phone in the recreation area and you refused to

wait on line to use it, I say. "Everything's changed," he says. You too? I say ecstatically.

10:19 A.M.: But it seems it doesn't have anything to do with Fuji moments. "I'm hooked in with this guy that's been in here nine times and he's like the Godfather of rehab," he says. "He can get you anything you need. Remember how I told you there's only one group TV and I couldn't get anybody to agree to watch my shows?" Yeah. "Well, we had A&E on all last night." What did you do, like give him cigarettes and stuff? "It's sort of like that but he doesn't smoke." Well? "He wanted this month's *GQ*."

10:41 A.M.: One of the supervisors is reading something in the paper about a meteor that could hit earth and calls everybody over to his desk to draw straws to see who gets to save the world. Marketing guy draws short straw.

10:42 A.M.: "We don't want to live in a world that has been saved by the marketing department," everyone says.

10:45 A.M.: Several workers start getting their affairs in order.

11:02 A.M.: One of the assistants tells everybody that one of her neighbors who had extensive liposuction came home from church all hysterical the other night. "They took the fat out of her knees," she says. "And she can't kneel and pray now. It's too painful. The cushioning is gone."

11:03 A.M.: "I tell you I don't know what they're doing with all that fat," Butty says. "At some point somebody's gonna do a big investigation piece and we're gonna find out where they've been dumping it all. It'll be like Love Canal, only Fat Canal."

11:18 A.M.: Rehab guy is back on the line. What, do you have your own phone now? I ask. "It's red," he says. "Anyway, remember how I told you the circles were making me dizzy? Every morning we're up at five forty-five and it's right into a group circle and then at ten it's another circle and eleven fifteen and on and on. All the therapists keep saying is 'Okay, let's circle up.' Well, tomorrow I get to say, 'Let's not.' Twice." Man, he got you out of group, I say. That is big. What'd you have to do? "Had the wife bring him Chick-Fil-A last night."

11:19 A.M.: "Oh, and he said I don't have to get up until six."

12:06 P.M.: Go to lunch and almost eat alone.

12:11 P.M.: Ultimate test. I wonder if today, even Taco Bell would look good to me. Go inside and explain to clerk that if I was to eat at Taco Bell for the first time in my life this would be the day, but I'm still kind of hesitant. "Why don't you read up on us first," she says, handing me a pamphlet. "Next."

12:12 P.M.: The Taco Bell Nutritional Guide. I can't believe this really exists. I sit down at table to look it over. Picture on cover looks good. The tomatoes are sweating. On top it says, "You'll Love It or We'll Eat It." What good would that do anybody?

12:15 P.M.: Good thing I don't have any food on the table taking up space because the pamphlet opens up like a road map into a big chart. According to the graph, the seven-layer burrito has 10 percent of the daily value of vitamin C based on a 2,000-calorie diet.

12:22 P.M.: Fascinated by the diabetic exchange section.

12:41 P.M.: Tempted by the Choc Taco, which is listed as having one gram of dietary fiber, but the idea of reading about food instead of actually eating any appeals to me more for some reason.

1:18 P.M.: Back at work, get called into big meeting to discuss our company's new vision for the future. I've sort of got a new vision myself, I tell the boss. But I'm not sure there's any future in it.

1:19 P.M.: You know, I'm always up for a meeting, but everybody in conference room is sitting in a big circle. You think we could square it off a little? I ask. It's making me dizzy.

2:02 P.M.: "What do you think of the plan we've got mapped out here?" boss asks me. To tell you the truth, sir, the way you've got it laid out there kind of reminds me of a Taco Bell Nutritional Guide.

2:41 P.M.: After meeting, coworker who's always been nice to me pulls me aside and says, "You're getting kind of loopy." I am not, I say. "You know I wouldn't say it if I didn't think there was definitely something wrong," she says. "You *are* getting loopy." Am not. "Are too."

2:41:51 P.M.: I am not, I said.

3:12 P.M.: Rehab guy calls. Wants me to pick up some sunblock and drop it off to him. "My rehab Corleone likes to sit outside in the courtyard but he doesn't like the generic crap the hospital here provides," he says. "He wants Johnson & Johnson." I'll see what I can do. What number does he want, 15? "I'm not sure, I'll get back to you after I watch *Talksoup.* One of the nurses told me we couldn't get E! but he confronted her for me." He confronted her about E!?

3:13 P.M.: "He confronted her about E!"

3:21 P.M.: Look down at my shoes. They look elegant and suave; hardly worn. They look like something out of *The King and I.* Stage shoes.

3:22 P.M.: I don't own a pair of stage shoes.

3:24 P.M.: What's this new medication doing to me? Am I losing all sense of reality? I don't want to be up walking around with a happy face and perceiving everything as shiny and new when in actuality I'm wearing tattered downtrodden shoes. We've got enough people like that walking around already and it's not pretty. I'd rather my outlook matched my shoes.

3:27 P.M.: Decide not to take my third pill today.

3:27:29 P.M.: And maybe not even my fourth.

3:31 P.M.: Coworker asks me if something is bothering me. "You look puzzled," she says. I'm just trying to match up my outlook with my shoes, I say.

4:51 P.M.: Phone mail message: "23."

5:02 P.M.: Things are starting to come back into focus so I stop by desk of coworker who felt I might be turning loopy to reassure her that's not the case. You know they try to get you to take this stuff to elevate your mood but there's certain things that shouldn't look good to you, I say. You know how close I came to eating Taco Bell today?

5:03 P.M.: Before heading out, make note in my journal: *Life isn't supposed to be a never-ending series of Fuji moments.*

5:38 P.M.: Stop at drugstore for sunscreen. Head over to cosmetic department. You don't look so great under fluorescent lights, I say to woman behind counter. Especially for a cosmetologist. "You're rude," she says.

5:39:39 P.M.: No, no. I've just stopped taking my medication.

DAY 26

We'll Always Have *Soul Train*

"People . . . they ain't no good."

—NICK CAVE

8:54 A.M.: "I can tell a person is lying just by looking at them," my wife says. I don't have that gift but I just assume everyone is lying, I say. "That works too," she says.

9:04 A.M.: Hear commentators talking on car radio about how our parents, having survived the Depression and getting credit for saving the world during World War II, are now being called the Greatest Generation. I wonder if we're the Worst Generation.

9:22 A.M.: Girl at minimart checkout is on the phone with her mother while she's slowly ringing up customers between remarks like, "But Mom, if she's going to act that way I'm not going to threaten her anymore. I'm going to go over to that bitch's house and kill her. Okay, Mom, I'll talk to you later."

9:26 A.M.: Were you really talking to your mother? I ask. "I'll tell you a secret," she says after the line lets up. "Whoever I'm talking to I call Mom so people in line don't complain. And if they do, someone else in line always says, 'Leave her alone. She's talking to her mother.'" You, I say, are part of the Worst Generation. "I know," she giggles, "isn't it awful?"

9:48 A.M.: In office lobby they're holding some kind of complimentary breakfast buffet. By the elevators I pass a group of about eighteen people all drinking sip-ups. They all must reach bottom at the same time because all the sudden there's this huge sucking sound and I'm pulled over to the other side of lobby like I'm caught in the backdraft of a semi. I've entered some kind of a sip-up vortex.

10:12 A.M.: Ask coworker if he thinks we're perhaps the worst of the Worst Generation. "Not quite," he says. "But if we hired a consultant, I'm sure he could suggest a few minor adjustments that would easily make us candidates for homecoming queen of the worst generation."

10:20 A.M.: One of our staff claims they don't want to be a team player anymore. "I just don't care anymore," she says. A veteran of many years explains to her how, in the eyes of management, not caring can make everyone seem even more like team players. "Deep down I don't give a crap as long as I get paid every two weeks so I just do whatever and merrily go along with anything the bosses want me to do whether it's stupid or not," he says. "I may have no integrity or pride in my work but on the surface that screams . . ."

10:21 A.M.: "Team player," everyone yells ecstatically.

11:01 A.M.: Cousin calls to confide to me that when he recently watched *The Horse Whisperer* on cable he was so riveted he refused to even get up to go to the bathroom. "I know it's supposed to be like a woman's movie but it was really good. A horse gets hit by a truck." Okay, thanks for keeping me informed, I say. "Wait, there's more . . ."

11:04 A.M.: I don't think I want to know anymore about your *Horse Whisperer*–watching experience, I say. "I wet my pants," he says. What? That is pitiful. "My girlfriend thought it was endearing that I would try to hold it during *The Horse Whisperer.* She doesn't know any other men that would do that." Of course she doesn't, I say. What kind of man wets his pants during *The Horse Whisperer*? You, my friend, are officially a card-carrying member of the Worst Generation.

11:07 A.M.: The guy by the window who never talks pipes up and says, "When I was a kid a bunch of us broke into this old guy's house and stole his rare coin collection and used it all at the arcade. I remember most of the coins were silver, really light, so even though I had about hundred quarters in my pockets my pants were barely falling down. The coins floated."

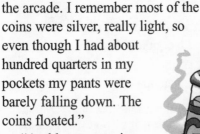

"And he gets a window seat," a worker who has a closet seat shouts. "That 'what goes around comes around' philosophy is bull."

11:10 A.M.: What does it tell us when a member of the Greatest Generation saves and treasures something only to have it stolen and squandered on pinball by the Worst Generation? If that doesn't illustrate what makes us the worst generation, I don't know what does.

11:11 A.M.: "I squandered his treasure on Frogger, not pinball," he says.

11:11:27 A.M.: You should just keep quiet, I say.

12:11 P.M.: Go to lunch and eat alone.

12:15 P.M.: Stop at credit union. "How's work going?" the teller asks. Deep down I don't give a crap, I say. On the surface, I'm a Team Player!

12:31 P.M.: Read about a football coach who just had quadruple bypass and I have to hope that he doesn't win any big games because I'm afraid he wouldn't survive getting a barrel of Gatorade dumped over his head, especially when the ice goes down his shirt and hits the spine. Ahh! In his condition, even a shoulder ride might be a stretch.

12:33 P.M.: Wonder if they could heat up some Gatorade, like a big NFL baby bottle.

12:35 P.M.: But what kind of generation would heat up Gatorade?

12:35:47 P.M.: The Worst.

12:36 P.M.: Exactly.

1:01 P.M.: Coworker is hyperventilating. Last night he got a ticket for littering when a flyer that was left under his windshield wiper blew off. "Why didn't you take it off before you got in the car?" someone asks. "I didn't want to touch it. It said *abs* on it. Something about how to get great abs."

1:02 P.M.: "Oooh, and you touched it?" everybody says. "No, I didn't touch it," he says. "That was the problem. And then when it flew off, the cop thought I'd thrown it out the window. I tried to explain that it was under my wiper blade. I didn't throw anything. But he said people like me don't want to be responsible for anything. He said I was responsible for what was under my wiper blades."

1:04 P.M.: "What's the number?" guy by closet shouts. "For what?" he says.

1:04:12 P.M.: "Great abs."

1:04:15 P.M.: "Go to hell."

1:04:33 P.M.: "You go to hell."

1:05 P.M.: Fighting among the ranks of the Worst Generation.

2:12 P.M.: Ex-ex-con houseguest calls me from his prison cell to let me know that number one, the prison dentist won't fix his front tooth. And number two, another inmate offered to help him wash his hair.

3:10 P.M.: Think about telling my wife I want a divorce when I get home but then I remember all my favorite shows are on tonight.

3:11 P.M.: It can wait.

3:12 P.M.: Wonder if a historian might list this kind of mentality—putting watching *Charmed* ahead of ending a marriage—as one of the classic attributes of the Worst Generation.

4:52 P.M.: I think I'm going to visit the convict in jail. Not to show any concern but just so I can put my hand up against the glass like they do in the movies, only just as he's about to line his palm up with mine I'm gonna pull it away real fast. *Gotcha.*

7:28 P.M.: When I get home, I catch the end of *Soul Train* and they're announcing that guests of the show stay at California's Nikko Hotel. Whenever you make reservations at the Nikko, be sure to ask for the *Soul Train* rate, they say.

7:30 P.M.: How cool would that be? To get the *Soul Train* rate. I have no intentions of going to Beverly Hills anytime soon but I call out to the Nikko just to see exactly how much the discount might be. I explain to the receptionist why I'm calling and she immediately puts me on hold.

7:31 P.M.: "Are you holding for the *Soul Train* rate?" a voice pops back on. Yes, yes I am.

7:31:51 P.M.: "Please hold."

7:32 P.M.: The Greatest Generation may have boldly survived the Depression, and the closest thing I may have experienced to what war feels like is a sip-up vortex, but I find it hard to be envious. My parents may have accomplished and experienced a hell of a lot, but I don't think they could even fathom a fraction of the thrill I'm feeling right now, holding on for the *Soul Train* rate . . . God bless this generation.

DAY 27

Rehearsal Time

"All I gotta do is act naturally."

—RINGO STARR

7:18 A.M.: Wake up very discouraged. Finally my dreams have been getting deeper and more meaningful but I just realized that the caliber of acting in my dreams is piss-poor. I tell my wife that I know my brain is supplying a good script but the actors in my dreams are treating it like bad dinner theater.

7:41 A.M.: While I eat breakfast I watch a videotape of *The Sopranos,* the Mafia soap opera on HBO. The head mob guy just got home from beating some snitch with a staple gun. He starts hyperventilating and collapses in his kitchen. Then he realizes he forgot to take his Prozac in the morning so he yells to his wife to bring him some. "Get your own goddamn Prozac!" she says. Why can't I get acting like this?

8:34 A.M.: While driving to work the steering wheel keeps pulling to the left. Is it my alignment or is the car trying to tell me to turn around and go home? Our temp-boss said anyone who worked last Saturday has to work this Saturday but that reasoning doesn't sound quite right to me.

9:46 A.M.: Security guard in parking lot is over by the bushes, where he must think nobody can see him, and he's doing these little bunny hops. He's sticking his butt out, putting his feet tightly together and hopping up and down off the foot-high curb, all the while keeping his hands on his hips so his keys don't rattle. It is very disturbing.

9:47 A.M.: As I approach I want to make myself invisible because no man should have to be caught in the act of doing something like this. But I can't and he catches me out of the corner of his eye in midhop and tries to contort it into something akin to an end-zone victory dance. Funny how someone would think that getting caught doing a victory dance in the bushes is less embarrassing than doing little bunny hops but I guess society dictates such standards.

9:47:22 A.M.: Anyway, as our eyes lock I give him the look that says: I am not judging you but if I was going to get caught doing something that I didn't want anyone to know about it would not be bunny hopping.

9:49 A.M.: See the happy lady on the way into building. "What's new in your world?" she says sprightly. My dreams are like bad dinner theater, I say. Even the extras suck.

10:18 A.M.: Several employees are upset that the boss wants them to smile when they answer the phone. "But no one can even see us," one worker says. "Exactly," the boss says.

11:03 A.M.: Ask new guy what he does when no one is looking. And keep in mind, I say, bunny hopping is taken.

11:04 A.M.: "You mean like something you wouldn't want to get caught doing but enjoy very much?" he says. Yes, exactly.

Ernest goes to Terry's Dream

TAKE 27

"Well, I like to do hand tricks," he says.

11:04:44 A.M.: Hand tricks?

11:05 A.M.: "Yeah, like this," he says, sticking his hands out and flipping them over the way Steve Martin used to do in that old King Tut dance. And then his hands become a blur and he starts singing: "It goes like this . . . everybody's doin' the hand jive . . . hmm babump hmm babump . . . everybody's doin' the hand jive."

11:06 A.M.: You shouldn't have shown me that, I say.

11:49 A.M.: Coworker says she can identify with my dream problem. "I had a dream last night and everyone just stood there," she says. "I'm like, are you people on the clock or what?"

12:01 P.M.: Try smiling when answering the phone but it's like that chewing-gum-and-walking-at-the-same-time thing.

12:11 P.M.: Go to lunch and eat alone.

12:40 P.M.: After eating try to take a little nap in my car, the thinking being that maybe the actors in my dreams just need a little more rehearsal time.

1:20 P.M.: Lady who looks like a disheveled TV anchor (her neckerchief seems to be going in one ear and coming out the other) gets off elevator on my floor and starts huffing and puffing. "And how is your day going?" she says.

1:20:18 P.M.: I've seen camp skits more polished than my dreams, I say.

2:12 P.M.: Ask receptionist what she does when no one is looking. And keep in mind, I say, bunny hopping and doing the hand jive are taken.

2:12:06 P.M.: Her phone rings but just before she picks it up she turns to me and says: "I'm not embarrassed about doing anything in front of anyone. I just don't want to smile when no one is looking."

4:10 P.M.: You know, those singing waiters and waitresses that put on a show after they give you your soup could do a better job in my dreams. I mean, I'm not asking for *Shakespeare in Love* performances but I'm getting *Ernest Goes to the Swap Shop*–caliber stuff.

4:13 P.M.: "All you're asking is for a decent ensemble cast," the coworker who understands says.

5:18 P.M.: On drive home the front wheels are pulling to the right now. Knowing what the alternative is, it must be the alignment.

8:15 P.M.: Watch the rest of *The Sopranos* on tape. Head mob guy is in a strip club reading an eldercare book because he just had to put his mother in an assisted-living facility in Jersey.

9:40 P.M.: Tell my wife I'm going to refuse to sleep until I sense that the actors in my dreams are going to at least try to be believable.

11:28 P.M.: Refuse to go to sleep.

11:34 P.M.: Go to sleep.

1:22 A.M.: Actor in dream is saying "Shoo" to a crowd of dumbfounded people but it's coming out like "Shoe." No inflection whatsoever. It's like he went to the school of antimethod acting. And, instead of looking chastised, the crowd has the universal expression of a child who's just been offered candy. I'm not usually one to interfere with my own dreams but this is ridiculous.

1:26 A.M.: "Cut!"

Day 28

Jesus Wore Hats?

"I'm lyin' in bed just like Brian Wilson did."

—BARENAKED LADIES

7:18 A.M.: Lying in bed and can't help thinking something's not right. "Just get up and maybe things will be different today," my wife says.

7:19 A.M.: That's never worked before, I say

7:20 A.M.: I should be on top of the world. Our ex-con is locked away, my pits are getting skinnier every day. Why aren't I on top of the world?

7:21 A.M.: Maybe it's because our temp-boss has reasoned that since we worked the last two Saturdays in a row we have to make it up by working this Sunday.

8:32 A.M.: On drive to work, I sense that I need to stop accepting things for what they are and start accepting things for what they aren't.

8:33 A.M.: Or something like that.

8:51 A.M.: Listening to sports station on the radio. I've acquired this strange habit of listening to people talk about sports but never actually watching any. I have never watched a college football game in my life but I listen attentively as the commentators talk about LSU's chances this weekend. "LSU stands a chance," the expert says.

8:52 A.M.: "Alabama and Auburn is a tough one to pick."

8:53 A.M.: "Clemson's got a rich tradition."

8:54 A.M.: Go back to seeing things for what they are.

9:12 A.M.: People seem curious about me today. Everyone is saying hello with a question. A former associate, who I know is now making a lot more money than me, catches me just getting out of the car. "Hey, what's going on?" she says. You're making more money than me, I say.

9:13 A.M.: Smoker out front nods and says, "How you doin'?" Actually, I say, I'm feeling a bit spiritual in a scientific sort of way.

9:14 A.M.: "Hey guy, what's happening?" the hey guy in the elevator asks me. You know those great ideas you have in the middle of the night that turn out to be lame when they hit the light of day? I say. I've got the reverse going on now.

10:22 A.M.: Boss is handing out another one of those "in lieu of pay raises" items with the company logo on it to build company unity and increase morale. It looks like a bulletproof vest.

10:23 A.M.: It is.

10:34 A.M.: Cubicle neighbor wants to tell me something "on the QT" but we're not sure what "QT" stands for. I think its origins are foreign, that it's like a British Intelligence term or French Intelligence, maybe. "I don't think there's any such thing as French Intelligence," he says.

10:50 A.M.: Coworker notices I'm gazing across the room. "What are you staring at?" she asks. I don't stare at things anymore, I stare into things, I say. "What are you staring into?" she says.

10:51 A.M.: The dart board.

11:52 A.M.: "You know, you're the type of person that needs a hobby even when they're at work," coworker says. "It doesn't seem like you have enough to do."

11:52:22 A.M.: Can I tell you something on the QT? I ask her. She's all ears.

11:53 A.M.: Lean in and whisper, LSU stands a chance.

11:58 A.M.: Brother in New York calls to tell me he was reading a magazine called *Sky Mall* on a plane and among all the things you could send away for was Jesus money. "And it's not a replica," he says. "It's the currency of the time." Jesus currency? How much? I ask. "Fifty-seven dollars." How could something two thousand years old be that cheap? I say. "Don't know," he says. "Maybe they have a lot of it." I don't think Jesus had much money, I say. What does it look like? "It looks like a big half-digested aspirin. I'm getting one. I'm gonna start collecting Jesus stuff. You want in? They send a catalog with other Jesus merchandise in it, too, like hats and stuff." I don't think Jesus wore hats, I say. I've never seen a picture of him with a hat on. "You in or not?" he says. I do need a hobby, I say, but let me think about it.

12:10 P.M.: Go to lunch and eat alone.

12:31 P.M.: Decide that if I think long enough I will come to the realization that something I've always believed to be true is actually false. I know it's a fact that I've been programmed to believe certain things in life.

12:34 P.M.: Can't think of anything.

12:37 P.M.: Woman in front of me at pizza place orders a slice of plain cheese pizza and when the guy behind the glass goes to lift up a slice from the tray she points and says, "No, that big one, right there."

12:37:44 P.M.: Guy makes a face. "Don't make a face at me," she says. "You cut them all different sizes and then act surprised when someone asks for the biggest one. Look at that skinny one next to it. It's half the size. It should be in an incubator, the poor thing."

12:38 P.M.: "Okay, Okay," the pizza guy says, serving up the big slice.

12:38:16 P.M.: Lady turns away and pizza guy looks at me like "look at what I have to put up with from these ditzy ladies." Don't make a face at me, I say. Don't cut them up like that and then make a face at me like I'm supposed to side with you, like we're supposed to get chummy because we're both in the man club. As far as I'm concerned, when it comes to the size of a slice, brotherhood ends. "Okay, Okay," he says, "what'll it be?"

12:39 P.M.: A slice of the mushroom, the big one, I say.

12:39:02 P.M.: Oh, don't act surprised.

1:15 P.M.: Atmosphere in office has heated up for some reason. One worker is calling another out into the hall to discuss a work-related problem that seems to have escalated rapidly. "We need to discuss this now. I mean now!" one says. "Come on, let's do it!" the other says. Only one puts the bulletproof vest on.

1:16 P.M.: Office toughs, I say, as the doors slam behind them. But, to be honest, I envy their passion. To be that passionate about your work would be magnificent. But, then again, if I got that wrapped up in my work I probably wouldn't have time for a hobby.

1:37 P.M.: "By the way, a hobby should be relaxing and fun," coworker tells me. "Most people would know that, but I thought I should tell you."

2:12 P.M.: Old neighbor calls from California to tell me he's wearing a wire now, but it's not like a Linda Tripp thing. "It's just to spy on myself," he says. "Things are happening so fast out here I thought I was missing stuff." Were you? "Yeah, but it's time-consuming when the first thing you do when you get home is replay the whole day," he says.

2:13 P.M.: "You ever just listen to your life?" he asks. No, I say. "I don't recommend it," he says.

3:10 P.M.: Read in paper that they asked some Super Bowl MVP running back what his hobby is and he said: "Sleeping."

3:11 P.M.: Because it's fun.

3:38 P.M.: Call from my younger brother in New York. "Hold on," he says. "One of the girls in the office knows about this religious stuff—I think it's her hobby or something. Here she comes, hold on, I want you to hear this from her. Here she is."

3:39 P.M.: "Jesus wore hats," a faint voice says.

5:01 P.M.: Put on bulletproof vest and head out.

5:07 P.M.: Smile at woman in lobby. She smiles back. Wonder if she's smiling with me or at me.

5:38 P.M.: On drive home stop and use gas station restroom. I've never so much as put a mark on a bathroom wall before and, for the most part, despise graffiti, but I just can't seem to help myself, and then I even step back to admire it: "Clemson's got a rich tradition."

6:18 P.M.: Going straight to bed, I tell my wife as soon as I get home. It's my new hobby. "When are you going to get back up?" she asks, a bit puzzled.

6:18:07 P.M.: When it stops being fun.

DAY 29

Hitchin' a Ride

"Another fork stuck in the road."

—GREEN DAY

6:10 A.M.: I'm ready. Car is in the shop so I was going to rent one but neighbor who works construction said he'd give me a ride because his crew is working downtown this week. "Just have to get up early. We get goin' early," he said.

6:15 A.M.: "You like getting up in the dark?" my neighbor asks as I get in the car. I was born in the dark, I say.

6:20 A.M.: "Just have to pick up Jerry," my neighbor says, going the opposite direction from where I work.

6:32 A.M.: Just have to wake up Jerry. He obviously doesn't like getting up in the dark.

6:48 A.M.: Jerry's in the car. But his tools aren't. "Just have to run by Ronnie's, my brother-in-law's, to pick up my tools," he says. "Make a left up here and then the third right and . . ."

7:10 A.M.: Just have to wake up Ronnie. "That's not going to be easy," Jerry says. My neighbor bangs on the front door, Jerry heads over to his bedroom window. I take the back. "Ronnie!" "Ronnie!" Ronnie!

7:20 A.M.: No Ronnie.

7:25 A.M.: "I think I can get into his garage," Jerry says. "Let me just have a cigarette and then we'll jimmy that door."

7:26 A.M.–7:45 A.M.: Watch Jerry and my neighbor smoke.

7:46 A.M.: Break into Ronnie's garage.

7:47 A.M.–8:20 A.M.: Look at stuff in Ronnie's garage. "These milk crates are from the early 1900s. He's going to make a table out of them," Jerry says. "Very Cracker Barrel," my neighbor says.

8:21 A.M.: Two young men on bicycles wearing white shirts and blue ties ride up the driveway. They ask if we have a moment. Jerry says, "Sure," invites them into the garage and starts showing them Ronnie's stuff. They're looking for a break in Jerry's tour so they can talk a little about the Lord, but Jerry's on a roll—describing tools, swinging from the electronic hoist, making them feel the wax finish on the hood of Ronnie's El Camino. He's turned the tide on religious door knockers. He's boring them to death.

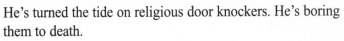

8:40 A.M.: They leave a pamphlet in one of the milk crates and pedal off.

8:41 A.M.: Wonder if I should have rode my bike the forty miles to work.

8:42 A.M.: Back in car.

8:43 A.M.: "I'm hungry," Jerry says.

9:20 A.M.: Microwave at 7-Eleven is broken but patrons are allowed to use the one in the break room of the adjacent auto parts store. "I've never been in their break room," Jerry says, meandering over. "Do you want a burrito?" he asks me. No thanks, I say. "It's not a regular burrito," he says. "It's a breakfast burrito."

9:49 A.M.: Back in car. "You sure you don't want a bite of this burrito," Jerry says. No, but I'll take a sip of that beer.

11:18 A.M.: Arrive at work. "You're late," the boss says. Got up early, I say.

11:27 A.M.: Office workers are discussing a baby that was found alive and healthy in a toilet at Disney World. "They named it Jasmine after the princess in Aladdin," one worker says. "That doesn't make sense," someone says. "They should have named it after Ariel, the Little Mermaid."

12:10 P.M.: Get a new company harassment policy in the mail. There's a list of nos, kind of like you'd see at a hotel pool. I've only had the list in my possession for a second but number five is already my favorite: No Taunting.

12:16 P.M.: Since I was late, I decide I should skip lunch today.

12:18 P.M.: A couple of masseuses are using the empty office next to ours to give once-a-week corporate massages to anyone who's interested. And a lot of people must be uptight this week because we're being overwhelmed by the fumes of Aspercreme or something that's wafting over. At first I welcomed the smell of Mentholatum to clear my sinuses but now it's making me so dizzy I can't seem to concentrate on anything but my work.

12:28 P.M.: Coworker wants to know if fish sticks is one word or two?

12:29 P.M.: Go to lunch and eat alone.

12:34 P.M.: The reason I eat alone isn't because I'm antisocial. I just hate to have anyone disturb me while I'm trying to concentrate on eating. I mean, I'm not like other people where I can sit and talk about a movie or Castro or garage sale permits or whatever and eat at the same time. I guess what I'm trying to say is: Eating does not come easy to me.

1:18 P.M.: By the time I get back to the office the air is so thick from the fallout of rubdown creams that phones are slipping out of people's hands. The entire staff is extremely loose and limber. "I just did a split," one coworker says.

1:20 P.M.: I feel like the one stick of spaghetti that didn't get into the pot. Rule number five is going out the window. People are sticking their tongues out at me and saying, "Bet you can't do this" as they poke their left feet into their right ears.

2:10 P.M.: My neighbor is on the phone. He's calling from the lobby. "Ready to go?" he says. What! It's only two o'clock, I say. "Come on," he says. "We've been at it since six."

2:11 P.M.: "Well?" he says.

2:12 P.M.: I'm thinking.

2:13 P.M.: "Hello . . . what's going on up there?"

2:13:06 P.M.: It's raining Ben Gay.

2:14 P.M.: "Just say your ride is here, you gotta go," my neighbor says. "People respect that. You can't keep your ride waiting. I hear people say that all the time—'I have to go. My ride's waiting.'"

2:14:13 P.M.: If ever there was a day custom-made for someone to slip out early, today is it.

2:15 P.M.: I have to go. My ride's waiting.

2:15:22 P.M.: On way out, notice that one worker has put a curtain around her cubicle and hung a small handwritten sign on the outside: SEE THE HUMAN CONTORTIONIST—50 CENTS."

2:19 P.M.: "Want a taco?" Jerry says, leaning over the front seat of the car. No thanks, I say, but I'll take a sip of that beer.

DAY 30

Fill 'er Up

"Doo-yoo-dee-dun-doo-yea . . .
Think about that."

—BOB MARLEY

7:39 A.M.: I feel empty. This is not good. This is when people get caught. You wake up on empty and the world sees you as extremely vulnerable. It wants to fill you up with fear or hatred or overpriced food at a theme restaurant. By the end of the day you're wearing nothing but a sheet over your head and a Planet Hollywood T-shirt.

7:44 A.M.: The little boy next door who's being raised by a single mom who works two jobs needs a ride to school. No can do. I'm too vulnerable. One ride with that kid and I'll be signing up to be a Big Brother, buying him Nintendo 64, coaching his soccer team . . . Before you know it I'm giving him his Tuesday-night baths and I'm up on molestation charges. "Okay, okay, I'll take him," my wife says.

8:38 A.M.: Guy on radio is talking about being filled up by Jesus. Jesus trying to enter me today would be like entering the wreck of the *Edmund Fitzgerald.* All he'd find is a shell and 98 percent water. Even he likes more of a challenge than that.

9:34 A.M.: I get on the elevator at the same time as a man in an army-green suit who looks like a comptroller. As we enter he walks right past the buttons and then says to me, "nineteen." He can sense he's in a confined space with a human vacuum and figures he can have his way with me. But even on empty I'm nobody's geisha boy. I dig deep and my left hand, which still has some pride left, pulls my right hand away from the button.

9:35 A.M.: The elevator isn't moving. Amidst the war of wills, I also forgot to press my own floor. The two of us are just sitting there.

9:36 A.M.: Doors open back onto lobby. I escape.

9:55 A.M.: Ask coworker what a comptroller is. I just used it in a sentence in my head but I don't know what it is, exactly. "It's a person who . . ." No, stop, I don't want to know. "But . . ." No! I never want to know. I made a vow to myself five years ago that I want to die not knowing what a comptroller is. "Then why'd you ask?" I'm sorry, I'm just weak today.

10:40 A.M.: Coworker in cubicle behind me (I've only seen the top of his head, like the guy on *Home Improvement*) points out that our office is filling up with too many workers who are frighteningly enthusiastic. Every encounter, every phone call is a blast of, "That's awesome! Are you kidding, that is so fantastic. Phenomenal. I love it, I love it, I love it." Every office has one of these people but it seems like they're almost outnumbering us here.

10:42 A.M.: We wonder if it is us, if we are lacking in our enthusiasm for life. "But don't you have to pick your moments?" he says. "A word like *awesome* is a standing-at-the-bottom-of-the-Grand-Canyon-looking-up kind of word. And they're using it to describe things like the remake of *Come On, Eileen.* I mean, what do they say when something big does happen? What do they call it when they have their first child, '*really* awesome'?"

11:38 A.M.: Wife calls to tell me she just realized that the only time she and her mother seem to be in sync anymore is at the Butterfly World theme park. That's nice, I say. Maybe we could have Thanksgiving there this year.

12:18 P.M.: Go to lunch and eat alone. Stuff myself but still feel empty. I've eaten a tuna kit, a bag of baby carrots, a generic Dr. Pepper called Dr. Thunder, and two Devil Dogs so I can't blame the feeling on Chinese food. Or can I?

12:43 P.M.: Check wrappers to see if Devil Dogs are made in China now.

1:20 P.M.: Phone call from my cousin whose wife is eight months pregnant. "We were all set to get an au pair but now my wife says she wants to get a nanny instead," he says. What's the difference? I ask. "I think it's dress size and age because the au pair I interviewed was twenty-two and about a size two and the nanny my wife likes is fifty-six and a Lane Bryant sixteen."

2:12 P.M.: There's a big commotion over at one of the enthusiastic people's desks. Someone is showing her something. There's a shriek that sounds sort of like information racing through a computer modem and then it's . . . "Oh, my God. That is fantastic. I can't believe . . . Where did you find it? Holy jeeze, it's wonderful. It's . . . it's superduper!"

2:13 P.M.: You've got to go over there and see what that person is showing her, I say over the border of my cubicle. We have to know how we'd react. "You go see," he says. I can't, I say. I'm too vulnerable.

2:14 P.M.: He quickly sashays over and then walks backward to the cubicle so I can't see his face. Well? Come on, what was it?

2:15 P.M.: "Wheat penny."

2:16 P.M.: Suddenly feel good about being empty. Fresh, like a trash can just lined with a brand-new twenty-gallon white tall kitchen bag ready to take whatever comes its way.

3:07 P.M.: A former associate calls from California. "Are you busy?" he says. As busy as an empty garbage can with a

brand-new bag, I say. "Whatever," he says, and rambles on
about how the new marketing company he's with is taking focus
groups to new heights. They're hypnotizing volunteers and taking them back to their childhoods, not to dig up traumatic events
but to dig up their first impressions of things like pudding.
"We're working on a campaign for a pudding company," he
says. "I'm even going to be one of the volunteers."

3:08 P.M.: I'd be careful, I tell him. You may just be going
back for pudding memories but other things could crop up.
Maybe your first pudding was with this Big Brother type who
promised you pudding after your Tuesday-night baths.

3:13 P.M.: Convict calls me from jail. Tells me he's being
released tomorrow. What?! I say. Don't tell me they're letting
you out for good behavior, anybody can behave for a couple of
days in prison. "Maybe they think I've learned my lesson," he
says. You son of a . . . "I'm just kidding, it just has something to
do with overcrowding," he says. "Anyway, can you pick me
up?"

3:14 P.M.: He must know he's catching me on the most vulnerable day of my life or he wouldn't even have the nerve to ask
me. Oh, why'd they even bother locking him up if they were
only going to keep him for a couple of days?

3:15 P.M.: "Well?" he says. I'm thinking I ain't no taxi service but the word *yes* just comes whimpering out of my mouth.

3:18 P.M.: Stare at the blinking cursor on my terminal for
what seems to be hours as I try to self-hypnotize myself back to
my first Freeze-a-Pop.

5:42 P.M.: Time to go.

6:13 P.M.: On way home stop at video store and fondle *The
English Patient* for about the tenth time in the past two years
and then put it back on the shelf. Hold it like a head of lettuce,
feel the sheer weight of it. I want to see it, but once again,
tonight's just not the night. Even though my brain is a barren

landscape I don't think I want it overflowing with three hours' worth of sand.

6:22 P.M.: Heading toward home I get the eerie feeling that something else might have preyed on my vulnerability today. It's like something's creeping up my shins, tripping over the splints, and heading toward my groin and gut, slowly trying to fill me up. It feels good but in a lame, superficial sort of way.

6:41 P.M.: My wife is in the driveway. "Hey, look," she says. "They finally dropped off that extra recycling bin we asked for."

6:42 P.M.: Awesome!

DAY 31

The Cost of Freedom

"When you think that you've lost everything you find out you can lose a little more."

—BOB DYLAN

7:19 A.M.: This is going to be the longest day of my life.

8:43 A.M.: On drive to work, I balance an article about Bob Dylan on steering wheel. In the interview he says, "I shut myself down when people come up and want to shake my hand or want to talk. That's just dead time."

9:22 A.M.: Hear on radio that when Hamas suicide bombers blow up Israeli buses they are not only promised martyrdom but a gift of seventy virgins from God when they arrive in heaven. I'm so relieved. I always thought they were bucking for some kind of higher plane that we mortals couldn't fathom and all this time it was just about sex. Can't wait to tell somebody.

9:58 A.M.: Tell security guard about the religious suicide bombers. "They do it for virgins?" the guard says. "I always thought they were on some kind of fundamental righteous higher ground that was incomprehensible to the rest of mankind." Nope, virgins, I say. It's no different than wanting to become a rock star. Everything is about sex, even blowing up buses in the name of God.

10:12 A.M.: New marketing person stops by my cubicle to introduce himself and reaches out to shake hands.

10:12:06 A.M.: Dead time.

10:44 A.M.: Get e-mail from guy in California. "I have an idea for a sitcom about a shrink who specializes in treating people who can't get a song out of their head," it says. "Each week it's a different song. Pilot episode: Aerosmith's *Walk This Way*."

10:45 A.M.: Walk this way . . .

11:14 A.M.: Boss wants to have a lunch meeting. One of those things where everyone gets takeout and sits around a big conference table. I protest. I'm extremely anti–lunch meetings. There's lunch and then there's meetings, I say. Two different things. "Twelve fifteen," boss says.

11:32 A.M.: Get phone call from a former associate in New York who has been trying to adopt a baby for about three years. "This one really looks like it could happen," he says. "But it's a stripper's baby. Don't get me wrong, she's one of the good-looking strippers, a high-class stripper. It's just . . . I don't know if I could love a stripper's baby."

11:33 A.M.: Walk this way . . .

11:40 A.M.: Copy of the company's new Zero Tolerance Policy lands on my desk. Zero tolerance for what? I ask the boss. "Everything," he says.

11:44 A.M.: Wonder if I could love a stripper's baby.

11:44:12 A.M.: I could.

12:20 P.M.: Go to lunch meeting but don't bring any food. It starts off with a lot of crunching. Croutons are loud.

12:31 P.M.: "I have an idea," somebody says. Hope it's a long one, everybody is thinking, so they can use the time to swallow.

12:43 P.M.: It is.

12:51 P.M.: Lunch meeting adjourned.

1:03 P.M.: Go to lunch and eat alone.

1:15 P.M.: Guy who works downstairs but always seems to be making the rounds is outside our office and wants to know if I have time for a twelve-minute story about his weekend. "I figure I tell it to seven or eight people and my day is over," he says. You plan that ahead of time? I ask. "With what they're paying me I'm 50 percent work, 50 percent talk now," he says proudly.

1:16 P.M.: I'm intrigued. Has the length become more important than the story itself? I ask. Do you sometimes intentionally stretch out spots and pause in places where there normally would be no pause just to eat up the clock? "Yeah, yeah, but you won't be able to tell," he says. "I've been doing this for a long time."

1:18 P.M.: Okay, shoot, I say.

1:30 P.M.: Good story, I say. And it came in right on schedule. But hey, that part about the garage-door opener where you stop and can't remember if it was your uncle or your grandfather who originally installed it and you're like rackin' your mind, is that for real or an artificial pause?

1:31 P.M.: "I've already wasted way too much time with you," he says, heading up the hallway.

1:39 P.M.: People always tell me I don't talk enough. I bet I'm only like 8 percent talk.

1:40 P.M.: But I'm certainly not 92 percent work. Where does the bulk of me go?

2:21 P.M.: Get postcard from coworker who went on vacation to New Orleans but never came back. His penmanship is very neat but he doesn't sound good. Says: "I'm having trouble with mirrors again. Sometimes I can't see myself. And the other day I tried leaving a phone message and nothing recorded. Friends say I'm looking better than ever. But they never knew ever."

3:10 P.M.: Art guy comes in with two eyeballs tattooed on the back of his head.

3:41 P.M.: Getting restless for this workday to end. "You look like you're getting itchy," coworker says.

3:51 P.M.: I wish I had a story to tell.

4:37 P.M.: Supposed to pick up convict early this evening so decide to head out.

7:40 P.M.: On TV watch *Inside the Actor's Studio.* The guest is Ron Howard and the host is thanking him for his body of work, for taking us from Mayberry to *Apollo 13,* from Opie to outer space. He says, "You're welcome."

10:39 P.M.: Waiting for another call from jail. First it was supposed to be eight o'clock, then nine, and now I've been napping on and off after he informed me they release prisoners after midnight because they want to get rid of them as soon as they've served a minute of the last day of their sentence. Can't you just stay until morning? I ask him. "No," he says. "They just kick you out in the middle of the night."

10:42 P.M.: I can't believe they just release all these convicts out into the night to roam the streets. Where do they go? What do they do?

10:50 P.M.: Watch another episode of *The Sopranos* and the family priest is telling the capo's wife that if they took everything Jesus ever said, it would only fill up a two-hour cassette. The capo's wife tells the priest that the Beatles only made a total of ten hours of music. "For real?" the priest says.

11:02 P.M.: Convict calls again to tell me it looks like it's going to be about one A.M. when he finally gets out. "I'm going to see if I can get a wake-up call," he says hanging up.

11:15 P.M.: "One in the morning? Are you sure you're not participating in a jail break?" my wife asks me.

11:16 P.M.: I hadn't thought of that.

11:23 P.M.: Call jail just to be sure I'm not the designated driver for a jail break and to check if they are really letting people out at one in the morning. "More like two," the woman says, hanging up.

11:24 P.M.: I can't believe I'm calling a jail like I call the airport to see what time a plane is arriving.

12:18 A.M.: Convict calls to tell me he's getting drowsy and would I mind if he reads me some poems he wrote. No, no prison poetry, I say. "Just listen to this one," he says. "'I exercise, I exercise, I exercise . . . I punch the air but slam my hand on bars and it hurts . . .' You like it? There's really no bars where I am, but I thought it sounded better than one-inch Plexiglas."

12:20 A.M.: Make myself some soup.

12:21 A.M.: Convict calls to tell me he can smell freedom. Really, I say. Does it smell anything like odorless eggs?

12:22 A.M.: "Did I tell you they gave me a number to a place that will fix my front tooth when I get out?" he says. "They said they would have to do it for free because I'm indignant," he says. I think you mean indigent, I say. "Whatever, I'm glad I'm it."

12:40 A.M.: Instead of waiting for more calls I decide to drive to the jail and just wait outside until they let him out.

12:53 A.M.: Park under a light.

1:04 A.M.: What am I doing here? I bet the highlights of my whole life could fit on one of those minicassettes that only has fifteen minutes on each side.

1:12 A.M.: Prisoners are starting to trickle out one by one. The first one heads directly toward me. "Got a cigarette?" he says. No, sorry, I say. I don't smoke.

1:14 A.M.: Second prisoner heads directly for me. "Got a cigarette?" he says.

1:16 A.M.: Third prisoner heads directly for me. "Got a cigarette?" he says.

1:17 A.M.: Go buy pack of cigarettes.

1:22 A.M.: "Got a cigarette?"

1:22:11 A.M.: Sure.

1:23 A.M.: "My moms was supposed to pick me up but she can't see good at night," he says, taking the cigarette and walking away.

1:27 A.M.: Guy I gave cigarette to is standing by exit now so everyone is approaching him for a cigarette. He shakes his head each time and then points to me. I'm giving them out like Halloween treats. This must be what it's like to be the most popular guy in the yard.

1:36 A.M.: One guy I give a cigarette to stands by my car window blowing smoke and asking me if I know what a good bowling ball costs. I have no idea, I say. "You're not the only one," he says.

1:42 A.M.: Another guy lingers to tell me that he's not worried about a job this time out because the Navy is desperate for help. "I saw this thing on CNN where they're even taking fat people now," he says.

1:42:28 A.M.: Where do you think all the fat goes when people get lipo? I ask.

1:42:34 A.M.: "They just need people to ride around on the ships," he says, ignoring my question. "Doesn't matter where you been or how much you weigh."

1:46 A.M.: Bowling-ball guy comes back for another cigarette. As I hand it over I have the opportunity to say what I've always dreamed of saying:

1:46:01 A.M.: That's my last one.

1:47 A.M.: But he doesn't say, "I can't take your last one," so the dream is not complete. Instead, he tells me how his uncle on the west coast sent him a bowling ball for Christmas, just before he got locked up, and he figures if he can sell it for a decent amount he wouldn't need to find work right away. "But I don't know what it's worth and nobody else seems to know either. Are you sure you don't know what a good bowling ball costs?" he says. I don't even know what a bad bowling ball costs, I say.

1:49 A.M.: He starts to walk away but then backtracks. "It cost my uncle twenty-two dollars just to ship it UPS. I still got the box to prove it," he says. Bowling balls are heavy, I say. But that's about all I know about them.

2:02 A.M.: Think I see my favorite prisoner coming out the gate, but he stops in a crowd and two other guys start to trail along with him. When he gets to the car he ducks in the window and asks if I can give his buds a ride. One of them is "My moms can't see good at night" and the other looks a lot like Dana Carvey, whom I haven't seen in a long time, so I say okay.

2:04 A.M.: We're just about to pull out when Dana says, "Damn, my belt buckle's not in with my stuff. The belt is here but they took the buckle off. Can you wait a second while I go get it from those bastards?"

2:05 A.M.: Wait for Dana to get belt buckle from those bastards.

2:11 A.M.: Still waiting for Dana to get belt buckle from those bastards.

2:14 A.M.: Ask my favorite prisoner how his stay was this time. "Lots of conversation," he says. You know, I say, everything Jesus ever said could fit on a two-hour tape. "Well, most people I met had a lot more to say than Jesus," he says.

2:15 A.M.: Sometimes, I say, especially when I'm picking up convicts in the middle of the night, I feel like the significance of everything I've done in my life so far could fit on someone's answering machine without even reaching the second beep. "That's heavy," the guy in the backseat says. "You wanna hear one of my poems?"

2:16 A.M.: "Oh, remember those old crummy sandals I had?" my favorite prisoner says, changing the subject slightly. "Look, I traded for Nikes." I turn the dome light on and sure as hell he's wearing brand-new Nikes.

2:16:47 A.M.: Turn dome light off.

2:17 A.M.: "When the guy in our quad asked me about trading, I had to freeze my expression," he says. "Because I knew he was debating it in his head. He wanted the sandals but he didn't want people to think he was a fool for trading his Nikes. So I put my Nikes-for-sandals?-Nothing-foolish-about-that expression on and just froze it."

2:18 A.M.: "And the guy threw in a pair of socks," he says, lifting his pant leg.

2:18:12 A.M.: Turn on dome light.

2:18:23 A.M.: See the Nike swoosh on his right sock.

2:19:33 A.M.: Turn off dome light.

2:24 A.M.: Dana gets back in car and says, "Got it."

2:25 A.M.: I tell the boys to buckle up and start the car just as the bowling guy pops his head in the passenger window and starts talking to my prisoner about how a bowling ball is like a microwave. "It looks nice, but you have no idea what it cost," he says. "I bet your driver there knows what a good bowling ball goes for . . ." Hey, I don't know squat about bowling balls, I yell. "All right, all right," he says, backing off.

2:27 A.M.: As we pull out toward the dark highway, I hit my high beams and floor it. The smell of dirt and freedom is in the air, and we're all off to a fresh start in a world where the possibilities are endless or, if not, you can always go home to your moms. Either way, the tape is rolling.

2:27:12 A.M.: "Got a cigarette?" Dana says.

2:28 A.M.: Walk this way . . .